HANDBOOK OF NATURE STUDY:

INSECTS

COMPLETE YOUR COLLECTION TODAY!

Reptiles, Amphibians, Fish and Invertebrates

Birds

Wildflowers, Weeds and Cultivated Crops

Mammals and Flowerless Plants

Trees and Garden Flowers

Earth and Sky

Insects

Introduction

Available at all online book retailers

or from livingbookpress.com

Handbook of Nature-Study:
Insects

ANNA BOTSFORD COMSTOCK, B.S., L.H.D

LATE PROFESSOR OF NATURE-STUDY IN CORNELL UNIVERSITY

All images are in the public domain unless otherwise credited.

If applicable the license is listed with the image credit. For full documentation on the licenses please visit-

GFDL 1.2
https://www.gnu.org/licenses/old-licenses/fdl-1.2.en.html

CC
https://creativecommons.org/licenses/

This edition published 2020
by Living Book Press

Copyright © Living Book Press, 2020

ISBN: 978-1-922348-62-3 (hardcover)
        978-1-922348-63-0 (softcover)

All rights reserved. No part of this publication may be reproduced, stored in a retrieval system, or transmitted in any other form or means – electronic, mechanical, photocopying, recording or otherwise, without the prior permission of the copyright owner and the publisher or as provided by Australian law.

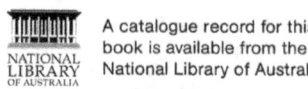

A catalogue record for this book is available from the National Library of Australia

CONTENTS

INSECTS

THE LIFE HISTORY OF INSECTS	3
THE STRUCTURE OF INSECTS	9
THE BLACK SWALLOW-TAIL BUTTERFLY	13
THE MONARCH BUTTERFLY	20
THE ISABELLA TIGER MOTH OR WOOLLY BEAR	28
THE CECROPIA	34
THE PROMETHEA	42
THE HUMMINGBIRD, OR SPHINX, MOTHS	47
THE CODLING MOTH	56
LEAF-MINERS	62
THE LEAF-ROLLERS	68
THE GALL-DWELLERS	72
THE GRASSHOPPER	79
THE KATYDID	87
THE BLACK CRICKET	91
THE SNOWY TREE-CRICKET	98
THE COCKROACH	101
THE DRAGON-FLIES AND DAMSEL-FLIES	107
THE CADDIS-WORMS AND THE CADDIS-FLIES	115
THE APHIDS, OR PLANT-LICE	122
THE ANT-LION	127
THE MOTHER LACE-WING AND THE APHIS-LION	131
THE MOSQUITO	135
THE HOUSE-FLY	144
THE COLORADO POTATO-BEETLE	151
THE LADYBIRD	156
THE FIREFLY	161

THE WAYS OF THE ANT	166
HOW TO MAKE THE LUBBOCK ANT-NEST	174
THE ANT-NEST, AND WHAT MAY BE SEEN WITHIN IT	176
THE MUD-DAUBER	184
THE YELLOW-JACKET	189
THE LEAF-CUTTER BEE	196
THE LITTLE CARPENTER-BEE	201
THE BUMBLEBEE	205
THE HONEY-BEE	210
THE HONEY-COMB	220
INDUSTRIES OF THE HIVE AND THE OBSERVATION HIVE	223

INSECTS

The Life History of Insects

INSECTS are among the most interesting and available of all living creatures for nature-study. The lives of many of them afford more interesting stories than are found in fairy lore; many of them show exquisite colors and, more than all, they are small and are, therefore, easily confined for observation.

While the young pupils should not be drilled in insect anatomy, as if they were embryo zoologists, yet it is necessary for the teacher, who would teach intelligently, to know something of the life stories, habits and structure of the common insects. Generally speaking, all insects develop from eggs. To most of us the word egg brings before us the picture of the egg of the hen or of some other bird. But insect eggs are often far more beautiful than those of any bird; they are of widely differing forms, and are often exquisitely colored and the shells may be ornately ribbed and pitted, sometimes adorned with spines, and are as beautiful to look at through a microscope as the most artistic piece of mosaic.

From the eggs, larvae *(sing. larva)* issue. These larvae may be cater-

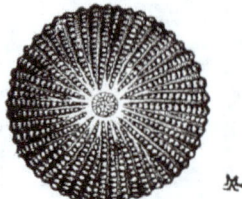 

The egg of the cotton moth, greatly enlarged.

pillars, or the creatures commonly called worms, or may be maggots or grubs. The larval stage is always devoted to feeding and to growth. It is the chief business of the larva to eat diligently and to attain maturity as soon as possible; for often the length of the larval period depends more upon food than upon lapse of time. All insects have their skeletons on the outside of the body; that is, the outer covering of the body is chitinous, and the soft and inner parts are attached to it and supported by it. This skin is so firm that it cannot stretch to accommodate the increasing size of the growing insect, thus from time to time it is shed. But before this is done, a new skin is formed beneath the old one. After the old skin bursts open and the insect crawls forth, the new skin is sufficiently soft and elastic to allow for the increase in the size of the insect. Soon, the new skin becomes hardened like the old

Caterpillar of the monarch butterfly

Butterfly chrysalis

one, and after a time, is shed. This shedding of the skin is called molting. Some insects shed their skins only four or five times during the period of attaining their growth, while other species may molt twenty times or more.

After the larva has attained its full growth, it changes its skin and its form, and becomes a pupa. The pupa stage is ordinarily one of inaction, except that very wonderful changes take place within the body itself. Usually the pupa has no power of moving around, but in many cases it can squirm somewhat, if disturbed. The pupa of the mosquito is active and is an exception to the rule. The pupa is usually an oblong object and seems to be without head, feet or wings; but if it is examined closely, especially in the case of butterflies and moths, the antennae, wings and legs may be seen, folded down beneath the pupa skin.

James Gathany (CC BY 2.5)
Mosquito larvae and one pupa, one of the only active pupa

A luna moth.
The delicate, exquisite green of the luna's wings is set off by the rose-purple, velvet border of the front wings, and the white fon on the body and inner edge of the hind wings. Little wonder that it has been called the "Empress of the night". The long swallow tail of the hind wings give the moth a most graceful shape, at the same time probably afford it protection from observation. During the day time the moth hangs wings down beneath the green leaves, and these long projections of the hind wings folded together resemble a petiole, making the insect look very much like a large leaf

Many larvae, especially those of moths, weave about themselves a covering of silk which serves to protect them from their enemies and the weather, during the helpless pupa period. This silken covering is called a cocoon. The larvae of butterflies do not make a silken cocoon, but the pupa is suspended to some object by a silken knob, and in some cases by a halter of silk, and remains entirely naked. The pupa of a butterfly is called a chrysalis. Care should be taken to have the children

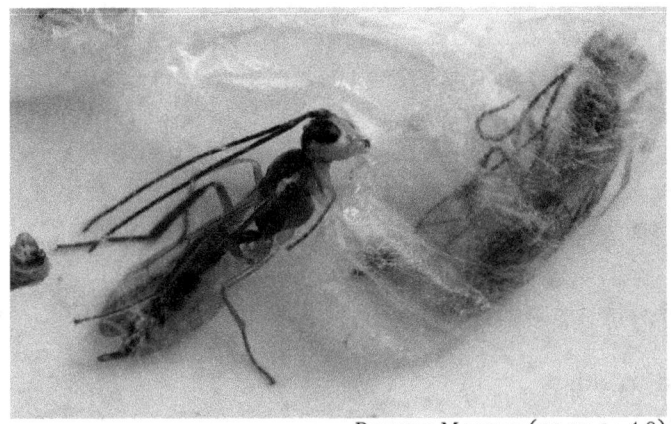

Beatriz Moisset (CC BY-SA 4.0)
An adult Ichneumonid wasp emerging from a cocoon

use the words—pupa, chrysalis and cocoon—understandingly.

After a period varying from days to months, depending upon the species of insect and the climate, the pupa skin bursts open and from it emerges the adult insect, often equipped with large and beautiful wings and always provided with six legs and a far more complex structure of body than characterized it as a larva. The insect never grows after it reaches this adult stage and, therefore, never molts. Some people seem to believe that a small fly will grow into a large fly, and a small beetle into a large beetle; but after an insect attains its perfect wings, it does not grow larger. Many adult insects take very little food, although some continue to eat in order to support life. The adult stage is ordinarily shorter than the larval stage; it seems a part of nature's economic plan that the grown-up insects should live only long enough to lay eggs, and thus secure the continuation of the species. Insects having the four distinct stages in their growth, egg, larva, pupa and adult, are said to undergo complete metamorphosis.

But not all insects pass through an inactive pupa stage. With some insects, like the grasshoppers, the young, as soon as they are hatched, resemble the adult forms in appearance. These insects, like the larvae, shed their skins to accommodate their growth, but they continue to

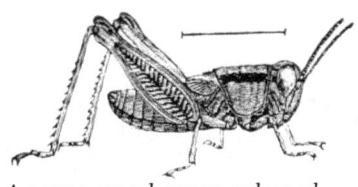

A young grasshopper, enlarged. The line shows its actual length

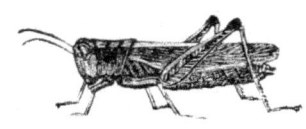

The adult of the same grasshopper, natural size

feed and move about actively until the final molt when the perfect insect appears. Such insects are said to have incomplete metamorphosis, which simply means that the form of the body of the adult insect is not greatly different from that of the young; the dragon-flies, crickets, grasshoppers and bugs are of this type. The young of insects with an incomplete metamorphosis are called nymphs instead of larvae.

Summary of the Metamorphoses of Insects

Complete Metamorphosis
- Egg.
- Larva.
- Pupa. (The pupa is sometimes enclosed in a cocoon.)
- Adult or winged insect.

Incomplete Metamorphosis
- Egg.
- Nymph (several stages).
- Adult, or imago.

Insect brownies; tree-hoppers as seen through a lens

The Structure of Insects

THE insect body is made up of ring-like segments which are grown together. These segments are divided into groups according to their use and the organs which they bear. Thus the segments of an insect's body are grouped into three regions, the head, the thorax and the abdomen. The head bears the eyes, the antennae, and the mouth-parts. On each side of the head of the adult insect may be seen the compound eyes; these are so called, because they are made up of many small eyes set together, much like the cells of the honeycomb. These compound eyes are not found in larvae. In addition to the compound eyes, many adult insects possess simple eyes; these are placed between the compound eyes and are usually three in number. Often they cannot be seen without the aid of a lens.

The antennae or feelers are composed of many segments and are inserted in front of the eyes or between them. They vary greatly in form. In some insects they are mere threads; in others, like the silk-worm moths, they are large, feather-like organs.

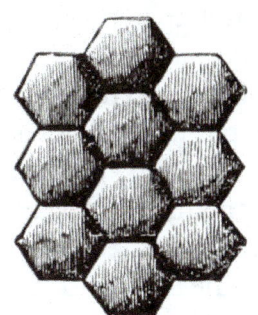

A part of the compound eye of an insect, enlarged

The mouth-parts of insects vary greatly in structure and in form, being adapted to the life of the insect species to which they minister. Some insects have jaws fitted for seizing their prey, others for chewing leaves, others have a sucking tube for getting the juices from plants

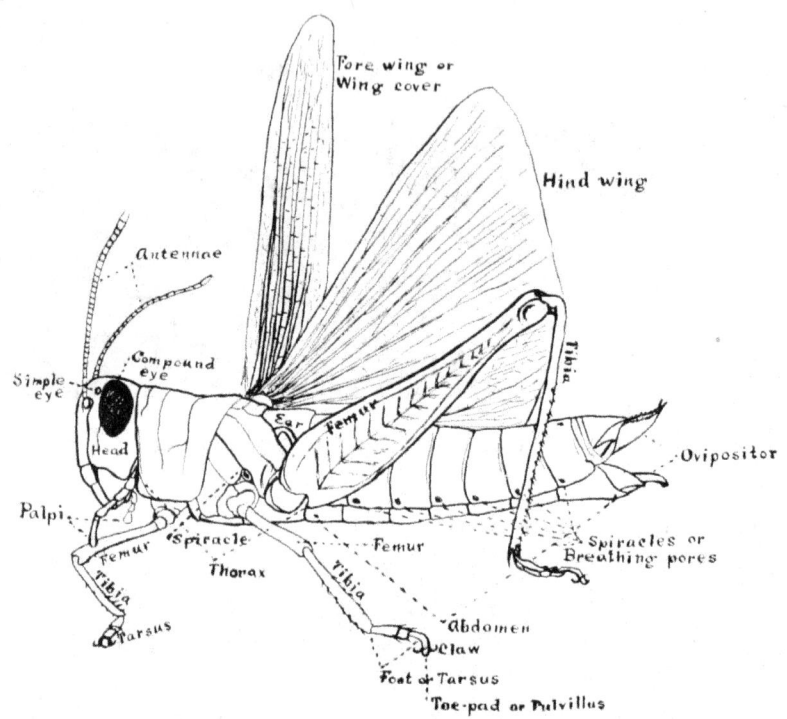

Grasshopper, with the parts of the external anatomy named

or the blood from animals, and others long delicate tubes for sipping the nectar from flowers.

In the biting insects, the mouth-parts consist of an upper lip, the labrum, and under lip, the labium, and two pairs of jaws between them. The upper pair of jaws is called the mandibles and the lower pair, the maxillae *(sing. maxilla)*. There may be also within the mouth, one or two tongue-like organs. Upon the maxillae and upon the lower lip there may also be feelers which are called palpi *(sing. palpus)*. The jaws of insects, when working, do not move up and down, as do ours, but move sidewise like shears. In many of the insects, the children are able to observe the mandibles and the palpi without the aid of a lens.

A tree hopper, showing the mouth as a long, three-jointed sucking tube, at a.

The thorax is the middle region of the insect body. It is composed of three of the body segments more or less firmly joined together. The segment next the head is called the prothorax, the middle one, the mesothorax, and the hind one, the metathorax. Each of these segments bears a pair of legs and, in the winged insects, the second and third segments bear the wings. Each leg consists of two small segments next to the body, next to them a longer segment, called the femur, beyond this a segment called the tibia, and beyond this the tarsus or foot. The tarsus is made up of a number of segments, varying from one to six, the most common number being five. The last segment of the tarsus usually bears one or two claws.

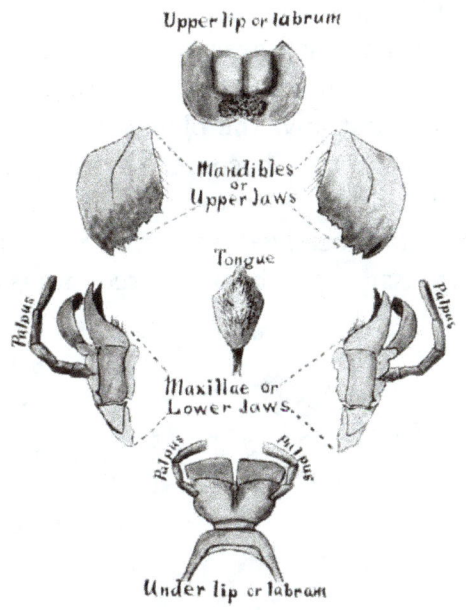

The mouth-parts of a grasshopper dissected off, enlarged and named.

While we have little to do with the internal anatomy of insects in elementary nature-study, the children should be taught something of the way that insects breathe. The child naturally believes that the insect, like himself, breathes through the mouth, while as a matter of fact, insects breathe through their sides. If we examine almost any insect carefully, we can find along the sides of the body a series of openings. These are called the spiracles, and through them the air passes into the insect's body. The number of spiracles varies greatly in different insects. There is, however, never more than one pair on a single segment of the body, and they do

A sphinx moth using its with its tongue unrolled into a flower

not occur on the head. The spiracles, or breathing pores, lead into a system of air tubes which are called tracheae (tra'-ke-ee), which permeate the insect's body and thus carry the air to every smallest part of its anatomy. The blood of the insect bathes these thin-walled air tubes and thus becomes purified, just as our blood becomes purified by bathing the air tubes of our lungs. Thus, although the insects do not have localized breathing organs, like our lungs, they have, if the expression may be permitted, lungs in every part of their little bodies.

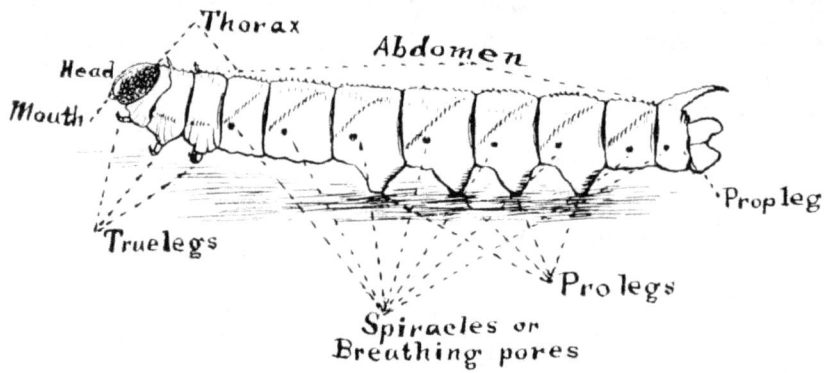

The sphinx caterpillar, with the parts of the external anatomy named

Head	{	Antennæ. Compound eyes. Simple eyes or ocelli.	
		Mouth-parts {	Labrum, or upper lip. Mandibles, or upper jaws. Maxillæ, or lower jaws, and maxillary palpi. Labium and labial palpi.
Thorax	{	Prothorax and first pair of legs.	
		Mesothorax and {	second pair of legs. first pair of wings.
		Metathorax and {	third pair of legs. second pair of wings.
		Wing {	veins. cells.
		Leg {	Two small segments called coxa and trochanter. Femur. Tibia. Tarsus and claws.
Abdomen	{	The abdomen bears {	ears (in locusts only). spiracles. ovipositor.

D. Gordon E. Robertson (CC BY-SA 3.0)
Male black swallowtail

The Black Swallow-Tail Butterfly

TEACHER'S STORY

THIS graceful butterfly is a very good friend to the flowers, being a most efficient pollen carrier. It haunts the gardens and sips nectar from all the blossom cups held out for its refreshment; and it is found throughout almost all parts of the United States. The grace of its appearance is much enhanced by the "swallow-tails," two projections from the hind margins of the hind wings. The wings are velvety black with three rows of yellow spots across them, the outer row being little crescents set in the margin of the wing; and each triplet of yellow spots is in the same cell of the wing between the same two veins. The hind wings are more elaborate, for between the two inside rows of yellow spots, there are exquisite metallic blue splashes, more vivid and more sharply outlined toward the inside of the wing and shading off to black at the outside. And just above the inner angle of the hind

Black swallowtail eggs on parsley

wing is an orange eye-spot with a black center. On the lower surface of the wings, most of the yellow spots are replaced with orange.

The mother butterfly is larger than her mate and has more blue on her wings, while he has the yellow markings of the hind wings much more conspicuous. She lays her egg, just the color of a drop of honey, on the under surface of the leaf of the food plant. After about ten days there hatches from this egg a spiny little fellow, black and angular, with a saddle-shaped, whitish blotch in the middle of its back. But it would take an elfin rider to sit in this warty, spiny saddle. The caterpillar has six spines on each segment, making six rows of spines, the whole length of the body; the spines on the black portions are black and those on the saddle white, but they all have orange-colored bases.

When little, spiny saddle-back gets ready to change its skin to one more commodious for its increased size, it seeks some convenient spot on the leaf or stem and spins a little silken carpet from the silk gland opening in its under lip; on this carpet it rests quietly for some time, and then the old tight skin splits down the back, the head portion coming off separately. Swelling out to fill its new skin to the utmost, it leaves its cast-off clothes clinging to the silken carpet and marches back to its supper.

But after one of these changes of skin it becomes a very different looking caterpillar, for now it is as smooth as it was formerly spiny; it is now brilliant caraway green, ornamented with roundwise stripes of velvety black; and set in the front margin of each of these stripes are six yellow spots. In shape, the caterpillar is larger toward the head; its true feet have little, sharp claws and look very different from the four pairs of prolegs and the hind prop-leg, all of which enable him to hold fast to the stem or the leaf; these fat legs are green, each ornamented with a black, velvety polka-dot.

When we were children we spent hours poking these interesting

Tracey Schiess (CC BY-SA 3.0)
Color variations in the black swallowtail caterpillar

creatures with straws to see them push forth their brilliant orange horns. We knew this was an act of resentment, but we did not realize that from these horns was exhaled the nauseating odor of caraway which greeted our nostrils. We incidentally discovered that they did not waste this odor upon each other, for once we saw two of the full-grown caterpillars meet on a caraway stem. Neither seemed to know that the other was there until they touched; then both drew back the head and butted each other like billy-goats, Whack! whack! Then both turned laboriously around and hurried off in a panic.

The scent organs of these caterpillars are really little Y-shaped pockets in the segment back of the head, pockets full of this peculiar caterpillar perfume. Under the stimulus of attack, the pocket is turned wrong side out and pushed far out making the "horns," and at the same time throwing the strong odor upon the air. This spoils the flavor of these caterpillars as bird food, so they live on in serene peace, never hiding under the leaves but trusting, like the skunk, to a peculiar power of repelling the enemy.

We must admire this caterpillar for the methodical way in which it eats the leaf: Beginning near the base, it does not burn its bridges behind it by eating through the midrib, but eats everything down to the midrib; after it arrives at the tip of the leaf it finishes midrib and all on

SDETWILER (CC BY-SA 4.0)
Black swallowtail chrysalis

its return journey, doing a clean job, and finishing everything as it moves along. (See *Moths and Butterflies*, Dickerson, p. 42.)

When the caterpillar has completed its growth, it is two inches long; it then seeks some sheltered spot, the lower edge of a clapboard or fence rail being a favorite place; it there spins a button of silk which it grasps firmly with its hind prop-leg, and then, with head up, or perhaps horizontal, it spins a strong loop or halter of silk, fastening each end of it firmly to the object on which it rests. It thrusts its head through, so that the halter acts as a sling holding the insect from falling. There it sheds its last caterpillar skin, which shrinks back around the button, revealing the chrysalis which is angular with ear-like projections in front. Then comes the critical moment, for the chrysalis lets go of the button with its caterpillar feet, and trusting to the sling for support, pushes off the shrunken skin just shed and inserts the hooks, with which it is furnished, firmly in the button of silk. Sometimes during this process, the chrysalis loses its hold entirely and falls to the ground, which is a fatal disaster. The chrysalis is yellowish brown and usually looks very much like the object to which it is attached, and is thus undoubtedly protected from sight of possible enemies. Then some day it breaks open, and from it issues a crumpled mass of very damp insect velvet, which soon expands into a beautiful butterfly.

References— *Everyday Butterflies*, Scudder; *Moths and Butterflies*, Dickerson; *How to Know the Butterflies*, Comstock; *Moths and Butterflies*, Ballard.

A female black swallowtail butterfly

LESSON

Leading thought— The caterpillars of the swallow-tail butterflies have scent organs near the head which they thrust forth when attacked, thus giving off a disagreeable odor which is nauseating to birds.

Method— In September, bring into the schoolroom and place in the terrarium, or breeding cage, a caraway or parsley plant on which these caterpillars are feeding, giving them fresh food day by day, and allow the pupils to observe them at recess and thus complete the lesson.

THE CATERPILLAR AND CHRYSALIS

Observations—

1. Touch the caterpillar on the head with a bit of grass. What does it do? What color are the horns? Where do they come from? Are there two separate horns or two branches of one horn? What odor comes from these horns? How does this protect the caterpillar? Does the caterpillar try to hide under the leaves when feeding? Is this evidence that

Side view of female swallowtail
Greg Hume (cc by-sa 3.0)

it is not afraid of birds?

2. Describe the caterpillar as follows: What is its shape? Is it larger toward the head or the rear end? What is its ground color? How is it striped? How many black stripes? How many yellow spots in each black stripe? Are the yellow spots in the middle, or at each edge of the stripe?

3. How do the front three pairs of legs look? How do they compare with the prolegs? How many prop-legs are there? What is the color of the prolegs? How are they marked? Describe the prop-leg. What is its use?

4. Observe the caterpillar eating a leaf. How does it manage so as not to waste any?

5. Have you found the egg from which the caterpillar came? What color is it? Where is it laid?

6. How does the young caterpillar look? What are its colors? How many fleshy spines has it on each segment? Are these white on the white segments and black on the black segments? What is the color of the spines at their base?

7. Watch one of these caterpillars shed its skin. How does it prepare for this? How does it spin its carpet? Where does the silk come from? Describe how it acts when shedding its skin.

8. When a caterpillar is full grown, how does it hang itself up to change to a chrysalis? How does it make the silk button? How does it weave the loop or halter? How does it fasten it? When the halter is woven what does the caterpillar do with it? Describe how the last caterpillar skin is shed. How does the insect use its loop or halter while getting free from the molted skin?

9. Describe the chrysalis. What is its general shape? What is its

color? Is it easily seen? Can you see where the wings are, within the chrysalis? How is the chrysalis supported?

10. How does the chrysalis look when the butterfly is about to emerge? Where does it break open? How does the butterfly look at first?

THE BUTTERFLY

1. Why is this butterfly called the black swallow-tail? What is the ground color of the wings? How many rows of yellow spots on the front wings? Are they all the same shape? How are they arranged between each two veins? Describe the hind wings. What colors are on them that are not on the front wings? Describe where this color is placed. Describe the eye-spot on the hind wing. Where is it? How do the markings on the lower side of the wing differ from those above? How does the ground color differ from the upper side?

2. What is the color of the body of the butterfly? Has it any marks? Has it the same number of legs as the Monarch? Describe its antennae. Watch the butterfly getting nectar from the petunia blossom and describe the tongue. Where is the tongue when not in use?

3. How does the butterfly pass the winter? How does the mother butterfly differ in size and in markings from her mate?

"The 'caraway worms' were the ones that revealed to us the mystery of the pupa and butterfly. We saw one climb up the side of a house, and watched it as with many slow, graceful movements of the head, it wove for itself the loop of silk which we called the 'swing' and which held it in place after it changed to a chrysalis. We wondered why such a brilliant caterpillar should change to such a dull-colored object, almost the color of the clapboard against which it hung. Then, one day, we found a damp, crumpled, black butterfly hanging to the empty chrysalis skin, its wings 'all mussed' as we termed it; and we gazed at it pityingly; but even as we gazed, the crumpled wings expanded and then there came to our childish minds a dim realization of the miracle wrought within that little, dingy, empty shell."

—HOW TO KNOW THE BUTTERFLIES, COMSTOCK.

The Monarch Butterfly

TEACHER'S STORY

IT IS a great advantage to an insect to have the bird problem eliminated, and the monarch butterfly enjoys this advantage to the utmost. Its method of flight proclaims it, for it drifts about in a lazy, leisurely manner, its glowing red making it like a gleaming jewel in the air, a very different flight indeed from the zigzag dodging movements of other butterflies. The monarch has an interesting race history. It is a native of tropic America, and has probably learned through some race instinct, that by following its food plant north with the opening season, it gains immunity from special enemies other than birds, which attack it in some stage in its native haunts. Each mother butterfly follows the spring northward as it advances, as far as she finds the milkweed sprouted. There she deposits her eggs, from which hatch individuals which carry on the migration as far to the north as possible. It usually arrives in New York State early in July. As cold weather approaches, the monarchs often gather in large flocks and move back to the South. How they find their way we cannot understand, since there are among them none of the individuals which pressed northward early in the season.

The very brilliant copper-red color of the upper sides of the wings of the monarch is made even more brilliant by the contrasting black markings which outline the veins and border the wings, and also cover the tips of the front wings with a triangular patch; this latter seems to be an especially planned background for showing off the pale orange and white dots set within it. There are white dots set, two pairs in two rows, between each two veins in the black margin of the wings; and the fringe at the edge of the wings shows corresponding white markings. The hind wings and the front portions of the front wings have, on their lower sides, a ground color of pale yellow, which makes the insect less conspicuous when it alights and folds its wings above its back, upper surfaces together. The black veins, on the lower surface of the hind wings, are outlined with white, and the white spots are much larger than on the upper surface. The body is black, ornamented with a few pairs of white spots above and with many large white dots below. The chief distinguishing characteristic of insects, is the presence of six legs; but in this butterfly, the front legs are so small that they scarcely look like legs.

It is easy to observe the long, coiled tongue of the butterfly. If the act is done gently, the tongue may be uncoiled by lifting it out with a pin. To see a butterfly feeding upon nectar, is a very interesting process and may be observed in the garden almost any day. I have also observed it indoors, by bringing in petunias and nasturtiums for my imprisoned butterflies, but they are not so likely to eat when in confinement. The antennae are about two-thirds as long as the body and each ends in a long knob; this knob, in some form, is what distinguishes the antennae of the butterflies from those of moths. The male monarch has a black spot upon one of the veins of the hind wing; this is a perfume pocket and is filled with what are called scent scales; these are scales of peculiar shape which cover the wing at this place and give forth an odor, which we with our coarse sense of smell cannot perceive; but the lady monarch is attracted by this odor. The male

PICCOLONAMEK (GFDL 1.2)
A monarch (left) and a viceroy (right) butterfly. Notice the black band on the hind wings of the viceroy that distinguish it from the monarch, which it imitates in color and markings.

monarch may be described to the children, as a dandy carrying a perfume pocket to attract his sweetheart.

It is very interesting to the pupils if they are able to see a bit of the butterfly's wing through a three-fourths objective; the covering of scales, arranged in such perfect rows, is very beautiful and also very wonderful. The children know that they get dust upon their fingers from butterflies' wings, and they should know that each grain of this dust is an exquisite scale with notched edges and a ribbed surface.

The monarch is, for some reason unknown to us, distasteful to birds, and its brilliant colors are an advertisement to all birds of discretion, that here is an insect which tastes most disagreeably and that, therefore, should be left severely alone, There is another butterfly called the viceroy, which has taken advantage of this immunity from bird attack on the part of the monarch and has imitated its colors in a truly remarkable way, differing from it only in being smaller in size and having a black band across the middle of the hind wing. (See The Ways of the Six Footed, "A Sheep in Wolf's Clothing").

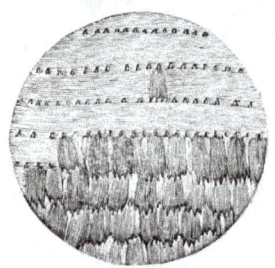

The scales on a butterfly's wing, as seen through a microscope

The milkweed caterpillar, which is the young of the monarch butterfly, is a striking object, and when fully grown is about two inches long. The milkweed is a succulent food and the caterpillar may mature in eleven days; it is a gay creature, with ground color of green and cross stripes of yellow and black. On top of the second segment, back of the head, are two long, slender whiplash-like organs, and on the seventh segment of the abdomen is a similar pair. When the caterpillar is frightened, the whiplashes at the front of the body twitch excitedly; when it walks, they move back and forth. Those at the rear of the body are more quiet and not so expressive of caterpillar emotions. These filaments are undoubtedly of use in frightening away the little parasitic flies, that lay their eggs upon the backs of caterpillars; these eggs hatch into little grubs that feed upon the internal fatty portions of the

Forest & Kim Starr (cc by-sa 3.0)
The monarch caterpillar

caterpillar and bring about its death through weakness. I remember well when I was a child, the creepy feeling with which I beheld these black and yellow-ringed caterpillars waving and lashing their whips back and forth after I had disturbed them; if the ichneumon flies were as frightened as I, the caterpillars were surely safe.

The caterpillar will feed upon no plant except milkweed; it feeds both day and night, with intervals of rest, and when resting, hides beneath the leaf. Its striking colors undoubtedly defend it from birds, because it is as distasteful to them as is the butterfly. However, when frightened, these caterpillars fall to the ground where their stripes make them very inconspicuous among the grass and thus perhaps save them from the attack of animals less fastidious than birds. These caterpillars, like all others, grow by shedding the skeleton skin as often as it becomes too tight.

The monarch chrysalis is, I maintain, the most beautiful gem in Nature's jewel casket; it is an oblong jewel of jade, darker at the upper end and shading to the most exquisite whitish green below; outlining

Greyson Orlando (CC BY 3.0)
Monarch chrysalis.
A jewel of living jade and gold.

this lower paler portion are shining flecks of gold. If we look at these gold flecks with a lens, we cannot but believe that they are bits of polished gold-foil. There may be other gold dots also, and outlining the apex of the jewel, is a band of gold with a dotted lower edge of jet; and the knob at the top, to which the silk which suspends the chrysalis is fastened, is also jet. The chrysalis changes to a darker blue-green after two days, and black dots appear in the gold garniture. As this chrysalis is usually hung to the under side of a fence rail or overhanging rock, or to a leaf, it is usually surrounded by green vegetation, so that its green color protects it from prying eyes. Yet it is hardly from birds that it hides; perhaps its little gilt buttons are a hint to birds that this jewel is not palatable. As it nears the time for the butterfly to emerge, the chrysalis changes to a duller and darker hue. The butterfly emerges about twelve days after the change to a chrysalis.

References— *Every Day Butterflies*, Scudder; *How to Know the Butterflies*, Comstock; *Moths and Butterflies*, Dickerson; *Ways of the Six Footed*, Comstock; *Moths and Butterflies*, Ballard.

Lesson

Leading thought— The monarch butterfly migrates northward, every spring and summer, moving up as fast as milkweed appears, so as to give food to its caterpillar; and it has often been noticed migrating back southward in the autumn in large swarms. This insect is distasteful to birds in all its stages. Its chrysalis is one of the most beautiful objects in all nature.

Method— This lesson should be given in September, while yet the caterpillars of the monarch may be found feeding upon milkweed, and while there are yet many specimens of this gorgeous butterfly to be seen. The caterpillars may be brought in, on the food plant, and their habits and performances studied in the schoolroom; but care should be taken not to have the atmosphere too dry.

Emerging from the chrysalis

THE BUTTERFLY

Observations—

1. How can you tell the monarch butterfly from all others? What part of the wings is red? What portions are black? What portions are white? What are the colors and markings on the lower side of the wings? What is the color of the body and how is it ornamented?

2. Is the flight of the monarch rapid or slow and leisurely? Is it a very showy insect when flying? Are its colors more brilliant in the sunshine when it is flying than at any other time? Why is it not afraid of birds?

3. When the butterfly alights, how does it hold its wings? Do you think it is as conspicuous when its wings are folded as when they are open?

4. Can you see the butterfly's tongue? Describe the antennae. How do they differ from the antennae of moths? How many legs has this butterfly? How does this differ from other insects? Note if you can see any indications of front legs.

5. Is there on the butterfly you are studying, a black spot near one of the veins on each hind wing? Do you know what this is? What is it for?

6. Why are the striking colors of this butterfly a great advantage to it? Do you know of any other butterfly which imitates it and thus gains an advantage?

A size comparison between similar caterpillars. Eastern black swallowtail (top), monarch (middle) and a queen (bottom)

THE MONARCH CATERPILLAR

1. Where did you find the monarch caterpillar? Was it feeding below or above on the leaves? Describe how it eats the milkweed leaf.

2. What are the colors and the markings of the caterpillar? Do you think these make it conspicuous?

3. How many whip-lash shaped filaments do you find on the caterpillar? On which segments are they situated? Do these move when the caterpillar walks or when it is disturbed? Of what use are they to the caterpillar?

4. Do you think this caterpillar would feed upon anything except milkweed? Does it rest, when not feeding, upon the upper or the lower surface of the leaves? Does it feed during the night as well as the day?

5. If disturbed, what does the caterpillar do? When it falls down among the grass how do its cross stripes protect it from observation?

6. Tell all the interesting things which you have seen this caterpillar do.

THE CHRYSALIS

1. When the caterpillar gets ready to change to a chrysalis what does it do? How does it hang up? Describe how it sheds its skin.

2. Describe the chrysalis. What is its color? How and where is it ornamented? Can you see, in the chrysalis, those parts which cover the wings of the future butterfly?

3. To what is the chrysalis attached? Is it in a position where it does not attract attention? How is it attached to the object?

4. After three or four days, how does the chrysalis change in color? Observe, if you can, the butterfly come out from the chrysalis, noting the following points: Where does the chrysalis skin open? How does the butterfly look when it first comes out? How does it act for the first two or three hours? How does the empty chrysalis skin look?

A BUTTERFLY AT SEA

Far out at sea-the sun was high,
  While veered the wind and flapped the sail;
We saw a snow-white butterfly
  Dancing before the fitful gale
    For out at sea.

The little wanderer, who had lost
  His way, of danger nothing knew;
Settled a while upon the mast;
  Then fluttered o'er the waters blue
    For out at sea.

Above, there gleamed the boundless sky;
  Beneath, the boundless ocean sheen;
Between them danced the butterfly,
  The spirit-life of this fair scene,
    Far out at sea.

The tiny soul that soared away,
  Seeking the clouds on fragile wings,
Lured by the brighter, purer ray
  Which hope's ecstatic morning brings—
    Far out at sea.

Away he sped, with shimmering glee,
  Scarce seen, now lost, yet onward borne!
Night comes with wind and rain, and he
  No more will dance before the morn,
    For out at sea.

He dies, unlike his mates, I ween,
  Perhaps not sooner or worse crossed;
And he hath felt and known and seen
  A larger life and hope, though lost
    Far out at sea.

—R. H. Horne.

ANDY REAGO & CHRISSY MCCLARREN (CC BY 2.0)

The Isabella Tiger Moth or Woolly Bear

TEACHER'S STORY

*"Brown and furry,
Caterpillar in a hurry,
Take your walk
To the shady leaf or stalk,
Or what not,
Which may be the chosen spot,
No toad spy you,
Hovering bird of prey pass by you;
Spin and die,
To live again a butterfly."*
—CHRISTINA ROSSETTI.

any times during autumn, the children find and bring in the very noticeable caterpillar which they call the "woolly bear." It seems to them a companion of the road and the sunshine; it usually seems in a hurry, and if the children know that it is hastening to secure some safe place in which to hide during the season of cold and snow, they are far more interested in its future fate. If the caterpillar is already curled up for the winter, it will "come to" if warmed in the hand or in the sunshine.

The woolly bear is variable in appearance; sometimes five of the front segments are black, four of the middle reddish brown, and three of the hind segments black. In others only four front segments are black, six are reddish, and two are black at the end of the body; there are still other variations, so that each individual will tell its own story of color. There are really thirteen segments in this caterpillar, not counting the head; but the last two are so joined that probably the children will count only twelve. There are a regular number of tubercles on each side of each segment, and from each of these arises a little rosette of hairs; but the tubercles are packed so closely together, that it is difficult for the children to see how many rosettes there are on each side. While the body of the caterpillar looks as if it were covered with evenly clipped fur, there are usually a few longer hairs on the rear segment.

There is a pair of true legs on each of the three front segments which form the thorax, and there are four pairs of prolegs. All of the segments behind the front three belong to the abdomen, and the prolegs are on the 3rd, 4th, 5th, and 6th abdominal segments; the prop-leg is at the rear end of the body. The true legs of this caterpillar have little claws, and are as shining as if encased in patent leather; but the prolegs and prop-leg are merely prolongations of the sides of the body to assist the insect in holding to the leaf. The yellow spot on either side of the first segment is a spiracle; this is an opening leading into the air tubes within the body, around which the blood flows and is thus purified. There are no spiracles on the second and third segments of the thorax, but eight of the abdominal segments have a spiracle on either side.

The woolly bear's head is polished black; its antennae are two tiny, yellow projections which can easily be seen with the naked eye. The eyes are too small to be thus seen; because of its minute eyes, the woolly bear cannot see very far and, therefore, it is obliged to feel its way. It does this by stretching out the front end of the body and reaching in every direction, to observe if there is anything to cling to in its neighborhood. When we try to seize the woolly bear it rolls up in a little ball, and the hairs are so elastic that we take it up with great difficulty. These hairs are a protection from the attacks of birds which do not like bristles for food; and when the caterpillar is safely rolled up, the bird sees only a little bundle of bristles and lets it alone. The woolly

Wooly bear   Micha L. Rieser

bear feeds upon many plants : grass, clover, dandelion, and others. It does not eat very much after we find it in autumn, because its growth is completed. The woolly bear should be kept in a box which should be placed out of doors, so that it may be protected from storms but have the ordinary winter temperature. Keeping it in a warm room during the winter often proves fatal.

Normally, the woolly bear does not make its cocoon until April or May. It finds some secluded spot in the fall, and there curls up in safety for the long winter nap; when the warm weather comes in the spring, it makes its cocoon by spinning silk about itself; in this silk are woven the hairs which it sheds easily at that time, and the whole cocoon seems made of felt. It seems amazing that such a large caterpillar can spin about itself and squeeze itself into such a small cocoon; and it is quite as amazing to see within the cocoon the smooth little pupa, in which is condensed all that was essential of the caterpillar. Sometimes when

Micha L. Rieser
The head of a wooly bear

the caterpillars are kept in a warm room they make their cocoons in the fall, but this is not natural.

The issuing of the moth from the cocoon is an interesting lesson for the last of May. The size of the moth which comes from the cocoon seems quite miraculous compared with the size of the caterpillar that went into it. The moth is in color dull, grayish, tawny yellow with a few black dots on the wings; sometimes the hind wings are tinted with dull orange-red. On the middle of the back of the moth's body there is a row of six black dots; and on each side of the body is a similar row. The legs are reddish above and tipped with black. The antennae are small and inconspicuous. The moths are night fliers, and the mother moth seeks some plant that will be suitable food for the little caterpillar as soon as it is hatched; here she lays her eggs.

Suggested reading — *Do You Know?* by Janet Smalley; *Nature by Seaside and Wayside,* by Mary G. Phillips and Julia M. Wright, Book 3, *Plants and Animals.*

Lesson

Leading thought — When we see the woolly bear hurrying along in the fall, it is hunting for some cozy place in which to pass the winter. It makes its cocoon, usually in early spring, of silk woven with its own hair. In late spring, it comes forth a yellowish moth with black dots on its wings.

Method — Have the children bring in woolly bears as they find them; place them in boxes or breeding jars which have grass or clover growing in them. The children can handle the caterpillars while they are studying them, and then they should be put back into the breeding jars and be set out of doors where they can have natural conditions; thus the entire history may be studied.

The Caterpillar

Observations — 1. How can you tell the woolly bear from all other caterpillars? Are they all colored alike? How many segments of the body are black at the front end? How many are red? How many segments are black at the rear end of the body? How many segments does this make in all?

Freshly laid (left) and mature (right) tiger moth eggs

2. Look closely at the hairs of the woolly bear. Are they set separately or in rosettes? Are any of the hairs of the body longer than others or are they all even?

3. Can you see, just back of the head, the true legs with their little sharp claws? How many are there?

4. Can you see the fleshy legs along the sides of the body? How many are there of these?

5. Can you see the prop-leg, or the hindmost leg of all? Of what use to the caterpillar are these fleshy legs?

6. Describe the woolly bear's head. How does it act when eating?

7. Can you see a small, bright yellow spot on each side of the segment just behind the head? What do you suppose this is? Can you see little openings along each side of all the segments of the body, except the second and third? What are they? Describe how the woolly bear breathes.

8. On what does the woolly bear feed? If you can find a little woolly bear, give it fresh grass to eat and see how it grows. Why does it shed its skin?

9. When the woolly bear is hurrying along, does it lift its head and

Isabella tiger moth with hindwings

the front end of its body now and then? Why does it do this? Do you think it can see far?

10. What does the woolly bear do when you try to pick it up? Do you find you can pick it up easily? Do you think that these stiff hairs protect the woolly bear from its enemies? What are its enemies?

11. Where should the woolly bear be kept in winter to make it comfortable?

The Cocoon

1. When does the woolly bear usually make its cocoon?

2. Of what material is it made? How does the woolly bear get into its cocoon?

3. What happens to it inside the cocoon?

4. Cut open a cocoon and describe how the woolly bear looks now.

The Moth

1. Where did the moth come from?

2. How did it come out of the cocoon? See if you can find the empty pupa case in the cocoon.

3. What is the color of the moth and how is it marked? Are the front and hind wings the same color?

4. What are the markings and colors of the body? Of the legs?

5. What do you think that the mother Isabella will do, if you give her liberty?

Kugamazog (cc by-sa 2.5)

Adult female cecropia moth

The Cecropia

Teacher's Story

THE silk-worm which gives us the silk of commerce, has been domesticated for centuries in China. Because of this domestication, it is willing to be handled and is reared successfully in captivity, and has thus come to be the source of most of our silken fabrics. However, we have in America native silk-worms which produce a silk that is stronger and makes a more lustrous cloth than does that made from the Chinese species. But we have never had the time and the patience, here in America, to domesticate these giant silk-worms of ours, and so they are, as yet, of no commercial importance.

The names of our common native silk-worms are: The cecropia, promethea, polyphemus, and luna. In all of these species the moths are large and beautiful, attracting the attention of everyone who sees them. The caterpillars are rarely found, since their varied green colors render them inconspicuous among leaves on which they feed. None of the caterpillars of the giant silk-worms occur in sufficient numbers to injure the foliage of our trees to any extent; they simply help nature to do a little needful pruning. All of the moths are night flyers and are, therefore, seldom seen except by those who are interested in the visitors to our street lights.

The cecropia is the largest of our giant silk-worms, the wings of the moth expanding sometimes six and one-half inches. It occurs from the Atlantic Coast to the Rocky Mountains.

The cecropia cocoon is found most abundantly on our orchard and shade trees; it is called by the children the "cradle cocoon," since it is shaped like a hammock and hung close below a branch, and it is a very safe shelter for the helpless creature within it. It is made of two walls of silk, the outer one being thick and paperlike and the inner one thin and firm; between these walls is a matting of loose silk, showing that the insect knows how to make a home that will protect it from winter weather. It is a clever builder in another respect, since at one end of the cocoon it spins the silk lengthwise instead of crosswise, thus making a valve through which the moth can push, when it issues in the spring. It is very interesting to watch one of these caterpillars spin its cocoon. It first makes a framework by stretching a few strands of silk, which it spins from a gland opening in the lower lip; it then makes a loose net-work upon the supporting strands, and then begins laying on the silk by moving its head back and forth, leaving the sticky thread in the shape of connecting M's or of figure 8's. Very industriously does it work, and after a short time it is so screened by the silk, that the rest of its performance remains to us a mystery. It is especially mysterious, since the inner wall of the cocoon encloses so small a cell that the caterpillar is obliged to compress itself in order to fit within it. This achievement would be something like that of a man who should build around himself a box only a few inches longer, wider and thicker than himself. After the cocoon is entirely finished, the caterpillar sheds its skin for the last time and changes into a pupa.

Very different, indeed, does the pupa look from the brilliant colored, warty caterpillar. It is compact, brown, oval and smooth, with ability to move but very little when disturbed. The cases which contain

The eggs of the cecropia moth

the wings, which are later to be the objects of our admiration, are now folded down like a tight cape around the body; and the antennae, like great feathers, are outlined just in front of the wing cases. There is nothing more wonderful in all nature than the changes which are worked within one of these little, brown pupa cases; for within it, processes go on which change the creature from a crawler among the leaves to a winged inhabitant of the air. When we see how helpless this pupa is, we can understand better how much the strong silken cocoon is needed for protection from enemies, as well as from inclement weather.

In spring, usually in May, after the leaves are well out on the trees, the pupa skin is shed in its turn, and out of it comes the wet and wrinkled moth, its wings all crumpled, its furry, soft body very untidy; but it is only because of this soft and crumpled state that it is able to push its way out through the narrow door into the outer world. It has, on each side of its body just back of the head, two little horny hooks that help it to work its way out. It is certainly a sorry object as it issues, looking as if it had been dipped in water and had been squeezed in an inconsiderate hand. But the wet wings soon spread, the bright antennae stretch out, the furry body becomes dry and fluffy, and the large moth appears in all its perfection. The ground color of the wings is a dusky, grayish brown while the outer margins are clay colored; the wings are crossed, beyond the middle, by a white band which has a broad outside margin of red. There is a red spot near the apex of the front wing, just outside of the zigzag white line; each wing bears, near its center, a crescent-shaped white spot bordered with red. But though it is so large, it does not need to eat; the caterpillar did all the eating that was necessary for the whole life of the insect; the mouth of the moth is not sufficiently perfected to take food.

Ceropia caterpillar — MICHAEL HODGE (CC BY 2.0)

When the cecropia caterpillar hatches from the egg, it is about a quarter of an inch long and is black; each segment is ornamented with six spiny tubercles. Like all other caterpillars, it has to grow by shedding its horny, skeleton skin, the soft skin beneath stretching to give more room at first, then finally hardening and being shed in its turn. This first molt of the cecropia caterpillar occurs about four days after it is hatched, and the caterpillar which issues looks quite different than it did before; it is now dull orange or yellow with black tubercles. After six or seven days more of feeding, the skin is again shed and now the caterpillar appears with a yellow body; the two tubercles on the top of each segment are now larger and more noticeable. They are blue on the first segment, large and orange-red on the second and third segments, and greenish blue with blackish spots and spines on all the other segments except the eleventh, which has on top, instead of a pair of tubercles, one large, yellow tubercle, ringed with black. The tubercles along the side of the insect are blue during this stage. The next molt occurs five or six days later; this time the caterpillar is bluish green in color, the large tubercles on the second and third segments being deep orange, those on the upper part of the other segments yellow, except those on the first and last segments, which are blue. All the other tubercles along the sides are blue. After the fourth molt it

CHARLES BENJAMIN SCHWAMB (CC BY-SA 3.0)
Newly emerged Cecropia hanging from a shrub

appears as an enormous caterpillar, often attaining the length of three inches, and is as large through as a man's thumb; its colors are the same as in the preceding stage. There is some variation in the colors of the tubercles on the caterpillars during these different molts; in the third stage, it has been observed that the tubercles, usually blue, are sometimes black. After the last molt the caterpillar eats voraciously for perhaps two weeks or longer and then begins to spin its cocoon.

References— Moths and Butterflies, Ballard; *Moths and Butterflies*, Dickerson; *Caterpillars and their Moths*, Elliot and Soule.

LESSON

Leading thought— The cecropia moth passes the winter as a pupa in a cocoon which the caterpillar builds out of silk for the purpose. In the spring the moth issues and lays her eggs on some tree, the leaves of which the caterpillar relishes. The caterpillars are large and green with beautiful blue and orange tubercles.

Method— It is best to begin with the cocoons, for these are easily found after the leaves have fallen. These cocoons if kept in the schoolroom should be thoroughly wet at least once a week. However, it is better to keep them in a box out of doors where they can have the advantage of natural moisture and temperature; and from those that are kept outside the moths will not issue, until the leaves open upon the trees and provide food for the young caterpillars when the eggs hatch.

MEGAN MCCARTY (CC BY-SA 3.0)
Cecropia pupa

THE COCOON

Observations—

1. How does the cocoon look on the outside? What is its general shape? To what is it fastened? Is it fastened to the lower or the upper side of a twig? Are there any dried leaves attached to it?

2. Where do you find cecropia cocoons? How do they look on the tree? Are they conspicuous?

3. Cut open the cocoon, being careful not to hurt the inmate. Can you see that it has an outer wall which is firm? What lies next to this? Describe the wall next to the pupa. How does this structure protect the pupa from changes of temperature and dampness?

4. Is the outside covering easy to tear? What birds are strong enough to tear this cocoon apart?

5. Are both ends of the cocoon alike? Do you find one end where the silk is not woven across but is placed lengthwise? Why is this so? Do you think that the moth can push out at this end better than at the other? Do you think the caterpillar, when it wove the cocoon, made it this way so that the moth could get out easily?

The Pupa

1. Take a pupa out of a cocoon carefully and place it on cotton in a wide-mouthed fruit jar where it may be observed. Can the pupa move at all? Is it unable to defend itself? Why does it not need to defend itself?

2. Can you see in the pupa the parts that will be the antennae and the mouth?

Shawn Hanrahan (CC BY-SA 2.5)
Young cecropia caterpillars

3. Describe how the wing coverings look. Count the rings in the abdomen.

4. Why does the pupa need to be protected by a cocoon?

The Moth

1. What is the first sign which you discover that the moth is coming out of the cocoon? Can you hear the little scratching noise? What do you suppose makes it? How does the moth look when it first comes out? If it were not all soft and wet how could it come out from so small an opening?

2. Describe how the crumpled wings spread out and dry. How does the covering of the wings change in looks?

3. Make a water-color drawing or describe in detail the fully expanded moth, showing the color and markings of wings, body and antennae.

4. Do the moths eat anything? Why do they not need to eat?

5. If one of the moths lays eggs, describe the eggs, noting color, size and the way they are placed.

The Caterpillar

1. On what do you find the cecropia caterpillar feeding? Describe its actions while feeding.

2. What is the color of the caterpillar? Describe how it is ornamented.

3. Can you see the breathing pores, or spiracles, along the sides of the body? How many of these on each segment? How do they help the caterpillar to breathe?

4. Describe the three pairs of true legs on the three segments just back of the head. Do these differ in form from the prolegs along the sides of the body? What is the special use of the prolegs? Describe the prop-leg which is the hindmost leg of all.

5. Do you know how many times the cecropia caterpillar sheds its skin while it is growing? Is it always the same color?

6. Watch the caterpillar spin its cocoon, describe how it begins and how it acts as long as you can see it. Where does the silk come from?

Kazvorpal (CC BY-SA 3.0)
Cecropia moths mating

JOMEGAT (CC BY-SA 3.0)

Female promethea moth
The Promethea

TEACHER'S STORY

THE promethea is not so large as the cecropia, although the female resembles the latter somewhat. It is the most common of all our giant silk-worms. Its caterpillars feed upon wild cherry, lilac, ash, sassafras, buttonwood and many other forest trees.

During the winter, leaves may often be seen hanging straight down from the branches of wild cherry, lilac and ash. If these leaves are examined, they will be found to be wrapped around a silken case containing the pupa of the promethea. It is certainly a canny insect which hides itself during the winter in so good a disguise, that only the very wisest of birds ever suspect its presence. When the promethea caterpillar begins to spin, it selects a leaf and covers the upper side with silk, then it covers the petiole with silk, fastening it with a strong band to the twig, so that not even most violent winter winds will be able to tear it off. Then it draws the two edges of the leaf about itself like a cloak as far as it will reach, and inside this folded leaf it makes its cocoon, which always has an opening in the shape of a conical valve at the upper end, through which the moth may emerge in the spring. This caterpillar knows more botany than some people do, for it makes no mistake in distinguishing a compound leaf from a simple one. When it uses a leaflet of hickory for its cocoon, it fastens the leaflet to the mid stem of the leaf and then fastens the stem to the twig. The male pupa is much more slender than that of the female. The moths do not issue until May or June.

The moth works its way out through the valve at the top of the cocoon. The female is a large, reddish brown moth with markings resembling somewhat those of the cecropia. The male is very different in appearance; its front wings have very graceful, prolonged tips, and both wings are almost black, bordered with ash color. The promethea moths differ somewhat in habit from the other silk-worms, in that they fly during the late afternoon as well as at night. The eggs are whitish with brown stain, and are laid in rows, a good many on the same leaf.

The caterpillars, as they hatch from the eggs, have bodies ringed with black and yellow. They are sociable little fellows and live together side by side amicably, not exactly "toeing the mark" like a spelling class, but all heads in a row at the edge of the leaf where each is eating as fast as possible. When they are small, the caterpillars remain on the under side of the leaves out of sight. In about five days, the first skin is shed and the color of the caterpillar remains about the same. Four or five days later, the second molt occurs, and then the caterpillar appears in a beautiful bluish green costume, with black tubercles, except four large ones on the second and third segments, and one large one on the eleventh segment, which are yellow. This caterpillar has an interesting habit of weaving a carpet of silk on which to change its skin; it seems to be better able to hold on while pushing off the old skin, if it has the silken rug to cling to. After the third molt, the color is a deeper greenish blue and the black tubercles are smaller, and the five big ones are larger and bright orange in color. After the fourth molt, which occurs after a period of about five or six days, the caterpillar appears in its last stage. It is now over two inches long, quite smooth and most

Promethea eggs and newly hatched caterpillars
Jacy Lucier (cc by-sa 4.0)

prosperous looking. Its color is a beautiful, light, greenish blue, and its head is yellow. It has six rows of short, round, black tubercles. The four large tubercles at the front end of the body are red, and the large tubercle on the rear end of the body is yellow.

The cynthia is a beautiful moth which has come to us from Asia; it is very large with a ground color of olive-green, with lavender tints and white markings; there are white tufts of hairs on the abdomen. It builds its cocoon like the promethea, fastening the petiole to the twig, therefore the lesson indicated for the promethea will serve as well for the cynthia. The cynthia caterpillars live upon the ailanthus tree and are found only in the regions where this tree has been introduced.

References— *Moths and Butterflies*, Dickerson; *Caterpillars and Their Moths*, Elliot and Soule; *Moths and Butterflies*, Ballard.

A promethea caterpillar
John Ghent (cc by 3.0)

Lesson

Leading thought— The promethea caterpillar fastens a leaf to a twig with silk and then makes its cocoon within this leaf. The male and female moths are very different in appearance.

Method— This work should begin in the late fall, when the children bring in these cocoons which they find dangling on the lilac bushes or wild cherry trees. Much attention should be paid to the way the leaf is fastened to the twig so it will not fall. The cocoons should be kept out of doors, so that the moths will issue late in the spring when they can have natural conditions for laying their eggs, and the young caterpillars are supplied with plenty of food consisting of new and tender leaves.

The Cocoon

Observations—

1. On what tree did you find it? Does it look like a cocoon? Does it not look like a dried leaf still clinging to the tree? Do you think that this disguise keeps the birds from attacking it? Do you know which birds are clever enough to see through this disguise?

2. How is the leaf fastened to the twig? Could you pull it off readily? What fastened the leaf to the twig?

3. Tear off the leaf and study the cocoon. Is there an opening to it? At which end? What is this for?

4. Cut open a cocoon. Is it as thick as that of the cecropia?

5. Study the pupa. Is it as large as that of the cecropia?

6. Can you see where the antennae of the moth are? Can you see the wing covers? Can the pupa move?

The Moth

1. Are there two kinds of moths that come from the promethea cocoons? Does one of them look something like the cecropia? This is the mother promethea.

2. Are any of the moths almost black in color with wings bordered with gray and with graceful prolonged tips to the front wings? This is the father moth.

3. Make water-color drawings of promethea moths, male and female.

4. If a promethea mother lays eggs, describe them.

The Caterpillar

1. How do the promethea caterpillars look when they first hatch from the eggs? Do they stay together when they are very young? How do they act? Where do they hide?

Male promethea moth

2. How do they change color as they grow older? Do they remain together or scatter? Do they continue to hide on the lower sides of leaves?

3. What preparation does a promethea caterpillar make before changing its skin? Why does it shed its skin? Do its colors change with every change of skin?

4. Describe the caterpillar when it is full-grown. What is its ground color? What are the colors of its ornamental tubercles? The color of its head?

5. Describe how a promethea caterpillar makes its cocoon.

DIDIER DESCOUENS (CC BY-SA 4.0)

Female hummingbird moth

The Hummingbird, or Sphinx, Moths

TEACHER'S STORY

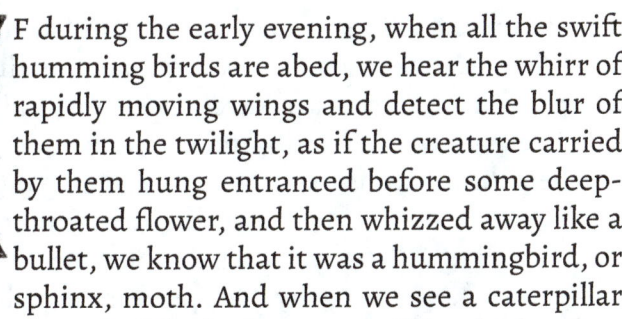

IF during the early evening, when all the swift humming birds are abed, we hear the whirr of rapidly moving wings and detect the blur of them in the twilight, as if the creature carried by them hung entranced before some deep-throated flower, and then whizzed away like a bullet, we know that it was a hummingbird, or sphinx, moth. And when we see a caterpillar with a horn on the wrong end of the body, a caterpillar which, when disturbed, rears threateningly, then we may know it is the sphinx larva. And when we find a strange, brown segmented shell, with a long jug handle at one side, buried in the earth as we spade up the garden in the spring, then we know we have the sphinx pupa.

The sphinx was a vaudeville person of ancient mythology who went about boring people by asking them riddles; and, if they could not

Didier Descouens (cc by-sa 4.0)
Male hummingbird moth

give the right answers, very promptly ate them up. Although Linnaeus gave the name of sphinx to these moths, because he fancied he saw a resemblance in the resting or threatening attitude of the larvae to the Egyptian Sphinx, there are still other resemblances. These insects present three riddles: The first one is, "Am I a humming bird?" the second, "Why do I wear a horn or an eye-spot on the rear end of my body where horns and eyes are surely useless?" and the third, "Why do I look like a jug with a handle and no spout?"

The sphinx moths are beautiful and elegant creatures. They have a distinctly tailor-made appearance, their colors are so genteel and "the cut" so perfect. They have long, rather narrow, strong wings which enable them to fly with extraordinary rapidity. The hind wings are shorter, but act as one with the front wings. The body is stout and spindle-shaped. The antennae are thickened in the middle or toward the tip, and in many species have the tip recurved into a hook. Their colors show most harmonious combinations and most exquisite contrasts; the pattern, although often complex, shows perfect refinement. Olive, tan, brown and ochre, black and yellow, and the whole gamut of greys, with eyespots or bands athwart the hind wings of rose color or crimson, are some of the sphinx color schemes.

Most of the sphinx moths have remarkable long tongues, being sometimes twice the length of the body. When not in use, the tongue is curled like a watch spring in front and beneath the head; but of what possible use is such a long tongue! That is a story for certain flowers to tell, the flowers which have the nectar wells far down at the base of tubular corollas, like the petunia, the morning glory or the nasturtium; such flowers were evidently developed to match the long-tongued insects. Some of these flowers, like the jimson weed and nicotina, open late in the day so as to be ready for these evening visitors. In some cases, especially in the orchids, there is a special partnership established between one species of flower and one species of sphinx moths. The tobacco sphinx is an instance of such partnership; this moth visits tobacco flowers and helps develop the seeds by carrying pollen from flower to flower; and in turn it lays its eggs upon the leaves of this plant, on which its great caterpillar feeds and waxes fat, and in high dudgeon often disputes the smoker's sole right to the "weed." Tobacco probably receives enough benefit from the ministrations of the moth to compensate for the injury it suffers from the caterpillars; but the owner of the tobacco field, not being a plant, does not look at it in this equitable manner.

The sphinx caterpillars are leaf eaters and each species feeds upon a limited number of plants which are usually related; for instance, one feeds upon both the potato and tomato; another upon the Virginia creeper and grapes. In color these caterpillars so resemble the leaves that they are discovered with difficulty. Those on the Virginia creeper, which shades porches, may be located by the black pellets of waste material which fall from them to the ground; but even after this unmistakable hint I have searched a long time to find the caterpillar in the leaves above; its color serves to hide the insect from birds which feed upon it eagerly. In some species, the caterpillars are ornamented

7 And (cc by-sa 3.0)
Pupa of the sphinx caterpillar
Note that the part encasing the long tongue is free and looks like the handle of a jug

with oblique stripes along the sides, and in others the stripes are lengthwise. There is often a great variation in color between the caterpillars of the same species; the tomato worm is sometimes green and sometimes black.

The horn on the rear end is often in the young larva of different color than the body; in some species it stands straight up and in some it is curled toward the back. It is an absolutely harmless projection and does not sting nor is it poisonous. However, it looks awe-inspiring and perhaps protects its owner in that way. The *Pandora* sphinx has its horn curled over its back in the young stage but when fully grown the horn is shed; in its place is an eyespot which, if seen between the leaves, is enough to frighten away any cautious bird fearing the evil eye of serpents. The sphinx caterpillars have a habit, when disturbed or when resting, of rearing up the front part of the body, telescoping the head back into the thoracic segments, which in most species are enlarged, and assuming a most threatening and ferocious aspect. If attacked they will swing sidewise, this way and then that, making a fierce crackling sound meanwhile, well calculated to fill the trespasser with terror. When resting they often remain in this lifted attitude for hours, absolutely rigid.

The six true legs are short with sharp, little claws. There are four pairs of fleshy prolegs, each foot being armed with hooks for holding on to leaf or twig; and the large, fleshy prop-leg on the rear segment is able to clasp a twig like a vise. All these fleshy legs are used for holding on, while the true legs are used for holding the edges of the leaf where the sidewise working jaws can cut it freely. These caterpillars do clean work, leaving only the harder and more woody ribs of the leaves. The myron caterpillar seems to go out of its way to cut off the stems of both the grape and Virginia creeper.

There are nine pairs of spiracles, a pair on each segment of the abdomen and on the first thoracic segment. The edges of these air openings are often strikingly colored. Through the spiracles the air is admitted into all the breathing tubes of the body around which the blood flows and is purified; no insect breathes through its mouth. These caterpillars, like all others, grow by shedding the skeleton skin, which splits down the back.

ERICM (CC BY-SA 3.0)
The sphinx caterpillar feeding on a tomato bush

Often one of these caterpillars is seen covered with white objects which the ignorant, who do not know that caterpillars never lay eggs, have called, eggs. But the sphinx moths at any stage would have horror of such eggs as these! They are not eggs but are little silken cocoons spun by the larvae of a hymenopterous parasite. It is a tiny, four-winged "fly" which lays its eggs within the caterpillar. The little grubs which hatch from these eggs feed upon the fleshy portions of the caterpillar until they get their growth, at which time the poor caterpillar is almost exhausted; and then they have the impudence to come out and spin their silken cocoons and fasten them to the back of their victim. Later, they cut a little lid to their silken cells which they lift up as they come out into the world to search for more caterpillars.

As soon as the sphinx larva has obtained its growth, it descends and burrows into the earth. It does not spin any cocoon but packs the soil into a smooth-walled cell in which it changes to a pupa. In the

EXILPATRIOT (CC BY-SA 4.0)
The caterpillar's rear can be easily mistaken for its face

spring the pupa works its way to the surface of the ground and the moth issues. In the case of the tomato and tobacco sphinx pupa, the enormously long tongue has its case separate from the body of the pupa, which makes the "jug handle." The wing cases and the antennae cases can be distinctly seen. In the case of the other species the pupae have the tongue case fast to the body. The larva of the Myron sphinx does not enter the ground, but draws a few leaves about it on the surface of the ground, fastens them with silk and there changes to a pupa.

References— Caterpillars and their Moths, Elliot and Soule; *Moths and Butterflies*, Dickerson; *Moths and Butterflies*, Ballard; *Manual for the Study of Insects*, Comstock.

LESSON

Leading thought— The sphinx caterpillars have a slender horn or eyespot on the last segment of the body. When disturbed or when resting they rear the front part of the body in a threatening attitude. They spin no cocoons but change to pupae in the ground. The adults are called hummingbird moths, because of their swift and purring flight. Many flowers depend upon the sphinx moths for carrying their pollen.

Method— The sphinx caterpillar found on the potato or tobacco, or one of the species feeding upon the Virginia creeper is in September available in almost any locality for this lesson. The caterpillars should be placed in a breeding cage in the schoolroom. Fresh food should be given them every day and moist earth be placed in the bottom of the cages. It is useless for the amateur to try to rear the adults from the pupae in breeding cages. The moths may be caught in nets during the evening when they are hovering over the petunia beds. These may be placed on leaves in a tumbler or jar for observation.

THE CATERPILLAR

Observations—

1. On what plant is it feeding? What is its general color? Is it striped? What colors in the stripes? Are they oblique or lengthwise stripes? Are all the caterpillars the same color?

2. Can you find the caterpillar easily when feeding? Why is it not conspicuous when on the plant? Of what use is this to the caterpillar?

JAMESDCARROLL (CC BY-SA 4.0)
A Myron caterpillar that has been parasitized. The white objects upon it are the cocoons of the little grubs which feed upon the fatty parts of the caterpillar

3. Note the horn on the end of the caterpillar. Is it straight or curled? Is it on the head end? What color is it? Do you think it is of any use to the caterpillar? Do you think it is a sting? If there is no horn, is there an eye-spot on the last segment? What color is it? Can you think of any way in which this eye-spot protects the caterpillar?

4. Which segments of the caterpillar are the largest? When the creature is disturbed what position does it assume? How does it move? What noise does it make? Do you think this attitude scares away enemies? What position does it assume when resting? Do you think that it resembles the Egyptian Sphinx when resting?

5. How many true legs has this caterpillar? How does it use them when feeding? How many prolegs has it? How are these fleshy legs used? How are they armed to hold fast to the leaf or twig? Describe the hind or prop-leg. How is it used?

A hummingbird clearwing extends its probiscus to feed from a flower

6. Do you see the breathing pores or spiracles along the sides of the body? How many are there? How are they colored? How does the caterpillar breathe? Do you think it can breathe through its mouth?

7. How does the sphinx caterpillar grow? Watch your caterpillar and see it shed its skin. Where does the old skin break open? How does the new, soft skin look? Do the young caterpillars resemble the full-grown ones?

8. Describe how the caterpillar eats. Can you see the jaws move? Does it eat up the plant clean as it goes?

9. Have you ever found the sphinx caterpillar covered with whitish, oval objects? What are these? Does the caterpillar look plump or emaciated? Explain what these objects are and how they came to be there.

10. Where does the caterpillar go to change to a pupa? Does it make cocoons? How does the pupa look? Can you see the long tongue case, the wing cases, the antennae cases?

The Moth

1. Where did you find this moth? Was it flying by daylight or in the dusk? How did its swift moving wings sound? Was it visiting flowers? What flowers? Where is the nectar in these flowers?

2. What is the shape of the moth's body? Is it stout or slender? What colors has it? How is it marked?

3. The wings of which pair are longer? Sketch or describe the form of the front and the hind wings. Are the outer edges scalloped, notched or even? What colors are on the front wing? On the hind one? Are these colors harmonious and beautiful? Make a sketch of the moth in watercolor.

4. What is the shape of the antennae? Describe the eyes. Can you see the coiled tongue? Uncoil it with a pin and note how long it is. Why does this moth need such a long tongue?

5. From what flowers do the sphinx moths get nectar? How does the moth support itself when probing for nectar? Do you know any flowers which are dependent on the sphinx moths for carrying their pollen? How many kinds of sphinx moths do you know?

Hurt no living thing:
Ladybird, nor butterfly,
Nor moth with dusty wing,
Nor cricket chirping cheerily,
Nor grasshopper so light of leap,
Nor dancing gnat, nor beetle fat,
Nor harmless worms that creep.

—Christina Rossetti.

Loniehuffman (CC BY 3.0)
Snowberry clearwing moth feeding on nectar

SIMON WINKLEY & KEN WALKER (CC BY 3.0)
Adult male (right) and female (left) codling moths

The Codling Moth

TEACHER'S STORY

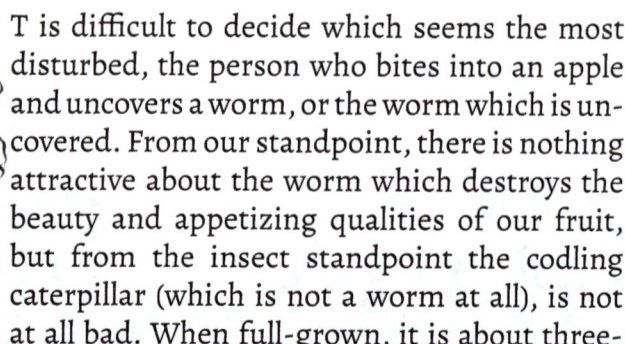

IT is difficult to decide which seems the most disturbed, the person who bites into an apple and uncovers a worm, or the worm which is uncovered. From our standpoint, there is nothing attractive about the worm which destroys the beauty and appetizing qualities of our fruit, but from the insect standpoint the codling caterpillar (which is not a worm at all), is not at all bad. When full-grown, it is about three-fourths of an inch long, and is likely to be flesh color, or even rose color, with brownish head; as a young larva, it has a number of darker rose spots on each segment and is whitish in color; the shield on the first segment behind the head, and that on the last segment of the body, are black. When full-grown, the apple worm is plump and lively; and while jerking angrily at being disturbed, we can see its true legs, one pair to each of the three segments of the body behind the head. These true legs have sharp, single claws. Behind these the third, fourth, fifth and sixth segments of the abdomen are each furnished with a pair of fleshy prolegs and the hind segment has a prop-leg. These fleshy legs are mere makeshifts on the part of the caterpillar for carrying the long body; since the three pairs of front legs are the ones from which develop the legs of the moth. The noticing of the legs of the codling moth is an important observation on the part of the pupils, since, by their presence, this insect may be distinguished from the young of the plum curculio, which is also found in apples but which is legless. The codling moth has twelve segments in the body, back of the head.

Codling moth larva in an apple

The codling larva usually enters the apple at the blossom end and tunnels down by the side of the core until it reaches the middle, before making its way out into the pulp. The larva weaves a web as it goes, but this is probably incidental, since many caterpillars spin silk as they go, "street yarn" our grandmothers might have called it. In this web are entangled the pellets of indigestible matter, making a very unsavory looking mass. The place of exit is usually circular, large enough to accommodate the body of the larva, and it leads out from a tunnel which may be a half inch or more in diameter beneath the rind. Often the larva makes the door sometime before it is ready to leave the apple, and plugs it with a mass of debris, fastened together with the silk. As it leaves the apple, the remnants of this plug may be seen streaming out of the opening. Often also, there is a mass of waste pellets pushed out by the young larva from its burrow, as it enters the apple; thus it injures the appearance of the apple, at both entrance and exit. If the apple has not received infection by lying next to another rotting apple, it first begins to rot around the burrow of the worm, especially near the place of exit.

The codling caterpillar injures the fruit in the following ways: The apples are likely to be stunted and fall early; the apples rot about the injured places and thus cannot be stored successfully; the apples thus injured look unattractive and, therefore, their market value is lessened; wormy apples, packed in barrels with others, rot and contaminate all the neighboring apples. This insect also attacks pears and sometimes peaches. It has been carefully estimated that every year

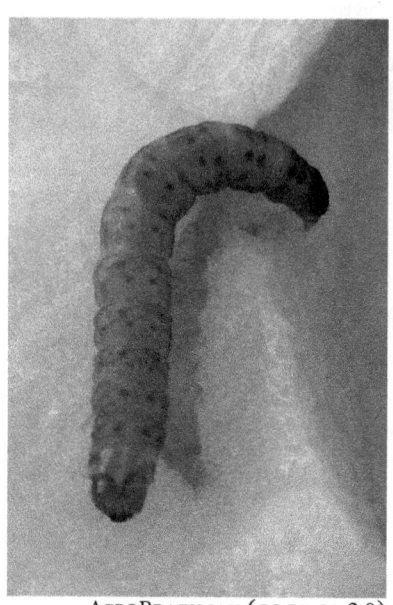
AfroBrazilian (cc by-sa 3.0)
Codling moth larva

the codling moth does three million dollars worth of injury to the apple and pear crops in New York State. Think of paying three million dollars a year for the sake of having wormy apples!

The larvae usually leave the apples before winter. If the apples have fallen, they crawl up the tree and there make their cocoons beneath the loose bark; but if they leave the apples while they are on the trees, they spin silk and swing down. If carried into the storeroom or placed in barrels, they seek quarters in protected crevices. In fact, while they particularly like the loose bark of the apple trees, they are likely to build their cocoons on nearby fences or on brush, wherever they can find the needed protection. The cocoon is made of fine but rather rough silk which is spun from a gland opening near the mouth of the caterpillar; the cocoon is not beautiful although it is smooth inside. It is usually spun between a loose bit of bark and the body of the tree; but after making it, the insect seems in no hurry to change its condition and remains a quite lively caterpillar until spring. It is while the codling larvae are in their winter quarters that our bird friends of the winter, the nuthatches, woodpeckers and chickadees, destroy them in great numbers, hunting eagerly for them in every crevice of the trees. It is therefore good policy for us to coax these birds to our orchards by placing beef fat on the branches and thus entice these little caterpillar hunters to visit the trees every day.

It is an interesting fact that the codling caterpillars, which make cocoons before August first, change immediately to pupae which soon change to moths, and thus another generation gets in its work before the apples are harvested.

The codling moth is a beautiful little creature with delicate antennae and a brown, mottled and banded body; its wings are graced by wavy bands of ashy and brown lines, and the tips of the front wings are dark brown with a pattern of gold bronze wrought into them; the hind wings are shiny brown with darker edges and little fringes. The moths issue in the spring and lay their eggs on the young apples just after the petals fall. The egg looks like a minute drop of dried milk and is laid on the side of the bud; but the little larva, soon after it is hatched, crawls to the blossom and finds entrance there; and it is therefore important that its first lunch should include a bit of arsenic and thus end its career before it fairly begins. The trees should be sprayed with some arsenical poison directly after the petals fall, and before the five lobes of the calyx close up around the stamens. If the trees are sprayed while blossoming, the pollen is washed away and the apples do not set; moreover, the bees which help us much in carrying pollen are killed. If the trees are sprayed directly after the calyx closes up around the stamens the poison does not lodge at the base of the stamens and the little rascals get into the apples without getting a dose. (See Lesson on the Apple).

Hectonichus (cc by-sa 3.0)
Pupa

Lesson

Leading thought— The codling moth is a tiny brown moth with bronze markings which lays its egg on the apple. The larva hatching from the egg enters the blossom end and feeds upon the pulp of the apple, injuring it greatly. After attaining its growth it leaves the apple and hides beneath the bark of the tree or in other protected places, and in the spring makes the cocoon from which the moth issues in time to lay eggs upon the young apples.

Method— The lesson should begin with a study of wormy apples, preferably in the fall when the worms are still within their burrows. After the pupils become familiar with the appearance of the insect and its methods of work, a prize of some sort might be offered for the one who will bring to school the greatest number of hibernating larvae found in their winter quarters. Place these larvae in a box with cheesecloth tacked over its open side; place this box out of doors in a protected position. Examine the cocoons to find the pupae about the last of April; after the pupae appear, look for the moths in about five days.

It would be a very good idea for the pupils to prepare a Riker mount showing specimens of the moths, of the cocoons showing the cast pupa skin, and of the caterpillar in a homeopathic vial of alcohol; pictures illustrating the work of the insect may be added. The pictures should be drawn by the pupils, showing the wormy apple, both the outside and in section. The pupils can also sketch, from the pictures here given, the young apple when just in the right condition to spray, with a note explaining why.

Observations—

1. Find an apple with a codling moth larva in it. How large is the worm? How does it act when disturbed?

2. What is the color of the caterpillar's body? Its head?

3. How many segments are there in the body? How many of these bear legs? What is the difference in form between the three front pairs of legs and the others?

4. Look at a wormy apple. How can you tell it is wormy from the outside? Can you see where the worm entered the apple? Was the burrow large or small at first? Can you find an apple with a worm in it which has the door for exit made, but closed with waste matter? How is this matter fastened together? If the apple has no worm in it, can you see where it left the apple? Make a sketch or describe the evidence of the caterpillar's progress through the apple. Do you find a web of silk in the wormy part? Why is this? Does the worm eat the seeds as well as the pulp of the apple?

5. Take a dozen rotting apples, how many of them are wormy? Do the parts of the apple injured by the worm begin to rot first? In how many ways does the codling moth injure the apple? Does it injure other fruits than apples?

6. How late in the fall do you find the codling larvae in the apple? Where do these larvae go when they leave the apple?

Work to be done in March or early April— Visit an orchard and look under the loose bark on old trees, or along protected sections of fences or brush piles and bring in all the cocoons you can find. Do not injure the cocoons by tearing them from the places where they are woven, but bring them in on bits of the bark or other material to which they are attached.

Olaf Leillinger (CC by-sa 2.5)

Adult codling moth

1. How does the cocoon look outside and inside? What is in the cocoon? Why was the cocoon made? When was it made?

2. Place the cocoons in a box covered with cheese-cloth and place the box out of doors where the contents can be frequently observed and make the following notes:

3. When does the larva change to the pupa? Describe the pupa. How does the cocoon look after the moth issues from it?

4. Describe the moth, noting color of head, thorax, body, front and hind wings.

5. If these moths were free to fly around the orchard, when and where would they lay their eggs?

6. When should the trees be sprayed to kill the young codling moth? With what should they be sprayed? Why should they not be sprayed during the blossoming period? Why not after the calyx closes?

7. How do the nuthatches, downy woodpeckers and chickadees help us in getting rid of the codling moth?

8. Write an essay on the life history of the codling moth, the damage done by it, and the best methods of keeping it in check.

References— The following bulletins from the U. S. Dept. of Agriculture: Farmers' Bulletin 247, "The Control of the Codling Moth and Apple Scab;" Bulletin 35, New Series, Bureau of Entomology, "Report on the Codling Moth Investigations," price 10 cents; Bulletin 41, "The Codling Moth," 105 pages, 15 cents, by Special Field Agent, C. B. Simpson; Bulletin 68, Part VII, "Demonstration Spraying for the Codling Moth," price 5 cents. The Spraying of Plants, Lodeman, Macmillan Company; Economic Entomology, Smith.

BEATRIZ MOISSET (CC BY-SA 4.0)   L. SHYAMAL (CC BY-SA 3.0)
Leaf miner path and larva

Leaf-Miners

TEACHER'S STORY

*"And there's never a leaf nor a blade too mean
To be some happy creature's palace".*

—LOWELL.

MAY not Lowell have had in mind, when he wrote these lines, the canny little creatures which find sustenance for their complete growth between the upper and lower surfaces of a leaf, which seems to us as thin as a sheet of paper. To most children, it seems quite incredible that there is anything between the upper and lower surfaces of a leaf, and this lesson should hinge on the fact that in every leaf, however thin, there are rows of cells containing the living substance of the leaf, with a wall above and a wall below to protect them. Some of the smaller insects have discovered this hidden treasure, which they mine while safely protected from sight, and thus make strange figures upon the leaves.

Among the most familiar of these are the serpentine mines, so called because the figure formed by the eating out of the green pulp of the leaf, curves like a serpent. These mines are made by the caterpillars of tiny moths, which have long fringes upon the hind wings. The life story of such a moth is as follows: The little moth, whose expanded wings measure scarcely a quarter of an inch across, lays an egg on the leaf; from this, there hatches a tiny caterpillar that soon eats its way into the midst of the leaf. In shape, the caterpillar is somewhat "square built," being rather stocky and wide for its length; it feeds upon the juicy tissues of the leaf and divides, as it goes, the upper from the lower surface of the leaf; and it teaches us, if we choose to look, that these outer walls of the leaf are thin, colorless, and paper-like. We can trace the whole life history and wanderings of the little creature, from the time when, as small as a pin point, it began to feed, until it attained its full growth. As it increased in size, its appetite grew larger also, and these two forces working together naturally enlarged its house. When finally the little miner gets its growth, it makes a rather larger and more commodious room at the end of its mine, which to us looks like the head of the serpent; here it changes to a pupa, perhaps after nibbling a hole with its sharp little jaws, so that when it changes to a soft, fluffy little moth with mouth unfitted for biting, it is able to escape. In some species, the caterpillar comes out of the mine and goes into the ground to change to a pupa. By holding up to the light a leaf thus mined, we can see why this little chap was never obliged to clean house; it mined out a new room every day, and left the sweepings in the abandoned mine behind. Mines of this sort are often seen on the leaves of nasturtium, the smooth pigweed, columbine, and many other plants. There are mines of many shapes, each form being made by a different species of insect. Some flare suddenly from a point and are trumpet-shaped while some are mere blotches. The blotch mines are made, through the habits of the insect within them; it feeds around and around, instead of forging

A serpentine mine in leaf of columbine

ahead, as is the case with the serpentine miners. The larvae of beetles, flies and moths may mine leaves, each species having its own special food plant. Most of the smaller leaf mines are made by the caterpillars of the moths, which are fitly called the Tineina or Tineids. Most of these barely have a wing expanse that will reach a quarter of an inch and many are much smaller; they all have narrow wings, the hind wings being mere threads bordered with beautiful fringes. The specific names of these moths usually end in "ella;" thus, the one that mines in apple is *malifoliella*, the one in grain is *granella*. One of these little moths,

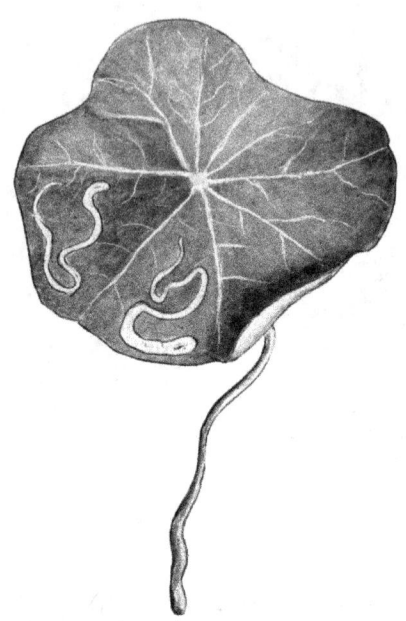

A serpentine mine in nasturtium leaf

Gelechia pinifoliella lives the whole of its growing life in half of a pine needle. The moth lays the egg at about the middle of the needle, and the little caterpillar that hatches from it, gnaws its way directly into the heart of the needle; and there, as snug as snug can be, it lives and feeds until it is almost a quarter of an inch long, think of it! Many a time I have held up to the light a pine needle thus inhabited, and have seen the little miner race up and down its abode as if it knew that something was happening. When it finally attains its growth it makes wider the little door, through which it entered; it does this very neatly, the door is an even oval, and looks as if it were made with the use of dividers. After thus opening the door, the caterpillar changes to a little, long pupa, very close to its exit; and later it emerges, as an exquisite little moth with silvery bands on its narrow, brown wings, and a luxurious fringe on the edges of its narrow, hind wings and also on the outer hind edges of the front wings.

The gross mines in the leaves of dock and beet are not pretty. The poor leaves are slitted, sometimes for their whole length, and soon turn brown and lie prone on the ground, or dangle pathetically from the stalk. These mines are made by the larvae of a fly, and a whole family live in the same habitation. If we hold a leaf thus mined up to the light, while it is still green, we can see several of the larvae working, each making a bag in the life substance of the leaf, and yet all joining together to make a great blister. The flies that do this mischief belong to the family *Anthomyinae;* and there are several species which have the perturbing habit of mining the leaves of beets and spinach. It behooves those of us who are fond of these "greens," as our New England ancestors called them, to hold every leaf up to the light before we put it into the skillet, lest we get more meat than vegetable in these viands. The flies, who thus take our greens ahead of us, are perhaps a little larger than house-flies, and are generally gray in color with the front of the head silver-white. These insects ought to teach us the value of clean culture in our gardens, since they also mine in the smooth pigweed.

Leaf miner trail on a fallen leaf

References— *Manual for the Study of Insects*, Comstock.

Lesson

Leading thought— The serpent-like markings and the blister-like blotches which we often see on leaves are made by the larvae of insects which complete their growth by feeding upon the inner living substance of the leaf.

Method— The nasturtium leaf-miner is perhaps the most available for this lesson since it may be found in its mine in early September. However, the pupils should bring to the schoolroom all the leaves with mines in them, that they can find and study the different forms.

Observations—

1. Sketch the leaf with the mine in it, showing the shape of the mine. What is the name of the plant on which the leaf grew?

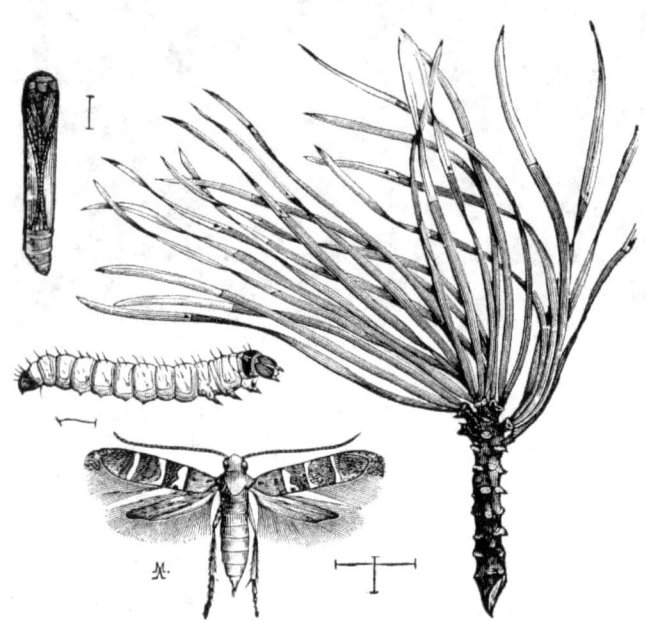

The pine-needle leaf-miner. The mined leaves of pine natural size. The caterpillar, pupa and moth of the leaf miner much enlarged. The lines show actual size of insect

2. Hold the leaf up to the light, can you see the insect within the mine? What is it doing? Are there more than one insect in the mine? Open the mine and see how the miner looks.

3. There are three general types of mines: Those that are long, curving lines called serpentine mines; those that begin small and flare out, called trumpet mines; and those that are blister-like called blotch mines. Which of these is the mine you are studying?

4. Study a serpentine mine. Note that where the little insect began to eat, the mine is small. Why does it widen from this point? What happened in the part which we call the serpent's head?

5. Look closely with a lens and find if there is a break above the mine in the upper surface of the leaf or below the mine in the lower surface of the leaf. If the insect is no longer in the mine can you find where it escaped? Can you find a shed pupa-skin in the "serpent's head?"

6. Why does an insect mine in a leaf? What does it find to eat? How is it protected from the birds or insects of prey while it is getting its growth?

7. Look on leaves of nasturtium, columbine, lamb's quarters, dock and burdock, for serpentine mines. Are the mines on these different plants alike? Do you suppose they are made by the same insect?

8. Look on leaves of dock, burdock, beet and spinach for blotch mines. Are there more than one insect in these mines? If the insects are present, hold the leaf out to the light and watch them eat.

9. Look in the leaves of pitch or other thick leaved pines (not white pine), for pine needles which are yellow at the tip. Examine these for miners. If the miner is not within, can you find the little circular door by which it escaped? Would you think there was enough substance in a half a pine needle to support a little creature while it grew up?

10. If you find leaf-miners at work, do not pluck off the leaves being mined but cover each with a little bag of swiss muslin tied close about the petiole and thus capture the winged insect.

Witch-hazel, showing work of leaf-rollers, leaf-miners and gall-makers.

The Leaf-Rollers

Teacher's Story

IF we look closely at sumac leaves before they are aflame from autumn's torch, we find many of the leaflets rolled into little cornucopias fastened with silk. The silk is not in a web, like that of the spider, but the strands are twisted together, hundreds of threads combined in one strong cable, and these are fastened from roll to leaf, like tent ropes. If we look at the young basswoods, we find perhaps many of their leaves cut across, and the flap made into a roll and likewise fastened with silken ropes. The witch-hazel, which is a veritable insect tenement, also shows these rolls. In fact, we may find them upon the leaves of almost any species of tree or shrub, and each of these rolls has its own special maker or indweller. Each species of insect, which rolls the leaves, is limited to the species of plant on which it is found; and one of these caterpillars would sooner starve than take a mouthful from a leaf of any other plant. Some people think that insects will eat anything that comes in their way; but of all created animals, insects are the most fastidious as to their food.

Some species of leaf-rollers unite several leaflets together, while others use a single leaf. In the case of the sumac leaf-roller, it begins in a single leaf; but in its later stages, it fastens

Leaf-rollers in sumac, with diagram showing the fastening of the silk stay ropes

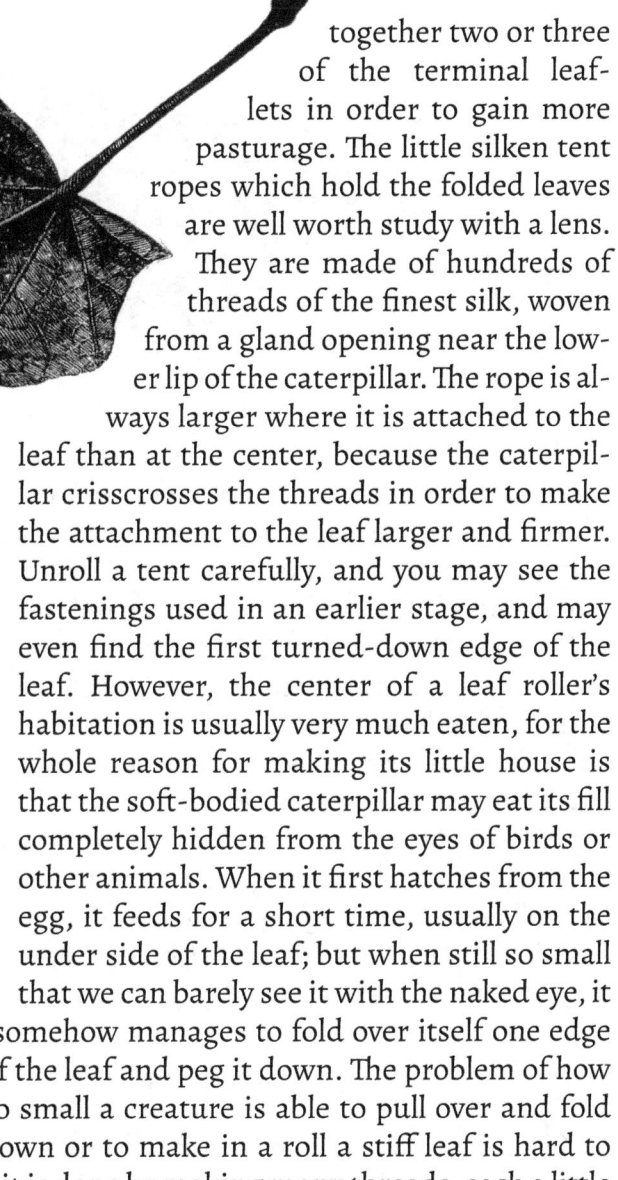

A leaf of basswood cut and rolled by the basswood leaf-roller

together two or three of the terminal leaflets in order to gain more pasturage. The little silken tent ropes which hold the folded leaves are well worth study with a lens. They are made of hundreds of threads of the finest silk, woven from a gland opening near the lower lip of the caterpillar. The rope is always larger where it is attached to the leaf than at the center, because the caterpillar crisscrosses the threads in order to make the attachment to the leaf larger and firmer. Unroll a tent carefully, and you may see the fastenings used in an earlier stage, and may even find the first turned-down edge of the leaf. However, the center of a leaf roller's habitation is usually very much eaten, for the whole reason for making its little house is that the soft-bodied caterpillar may eat its fill completely hidden from the eyes of birds or other animals. When it first hatches from the egg, it feeds for a short time, usually on the under side of the leaf; but when still so small that we can barely see it with the naked eye, it somehow manages to fold over itself one edge of the leaf and peg it down. The problem of how so small a creature is able to pull over and fold down or to make in a roll a stiff leaf is hard to solve. I, myself, believe it is done by making many threads, each a little more taut than the last. I have watched several species working, and the leaf comes slowly together as the caterpillar stretches its head and sways back and forth hundreds of times, fastening the silk first to one side and then to the other. Some observers believe that the caterpillar throws its weight upon the silk, in order to pull the leaf together; but

Leaflets of locust, fastened together to make a nest by the caterpillar of a butterfly

in the case of the sumac leaf-roller, I am sure this is not true, as I have watched the process again and again under a lens, and could detect no signs of this method. Many of the caterpillars which make rolls, change to small moths known as Tortricids. This is a very large family, containing a vast number of species and not all of the members are leaf-rollers. These little moths have the front wings rather wide and more or less rectangular in outline. The entomologists have a pleasing fashion of ending the names of all of these moths with "ana;" the one that rolls the currant leaves is *Rosana*, the one on juniper is *Rutilana*, etc. Since many of the caterpillars of this family seek the ground to pupate and do not appear as moths until the following spring, it is somewhat difficult to study their complete life histories, unless one has well-made breeding cages with earth at the bottom; and even then it is difficult to keep them under natural conditions, since in an ordinary living room the insects dry up and do not mature.

Lesson

Leading thought— There are many kinds of insects which roll the leaves of trees and plants into tents, in which they dwell and feed during their early stages.

Method— This is an excellent lesson for early autumn when the pupils may find many of these rolled leaves, which they may bring to the schoolroom, and which will give material for the lesson. The rolls are found plentifully on sumac, basswood and witch-hazel.

Observations—

1. What is the name of the trees and shrubs from which these rolled leaves which you have collected were taken?

2. Are more than one leaf or leaflet used in making the roll?

3. Is the leaf rolled crosswise or lengthwise? How large is the tube thus made?

4. Is the nest in the shape of a tube, or are several leaves fastened together, making a box-shaped nest?

5. How is the roll made fast? Examine the little silken ropes with a lens and describe one of them. Is it wider where it is attached to the leaf than at the middle? Why?

6. How many of these tent ropes are there which make fast the roll? Unroll a leaf carefully and see if you can find signs of the tent ropes that fastened the roll together when it was smaller. Can you find where it began?

7. As you unroll the leaves what do you see at the center? Has the leaf been eaten? Can you discover the reason why the caterpillar made this roll?

8. How do you think a caterpillar manages to roll a leaf so successfully? Where is the spinning gland of a caterpillar? How does the insect act when spinning threads back and forth when rolling the leaf? What sort of insect does the caterpillar which rolls the leaf change into? Do you suppose that the same kind of caterpillars makes the rolls on two different species of trees?

9. In July or early August get some of the rolls with the caterpillars in them, unroll a nest, take the caterpillar out and put it on a fresh leaf of the same kind of tree or shrub on which you found it, and watch it make its roll.

Supplementary reading— "A Dweller in Tents" and "A Little Nomad," in *Ways of the Six-Footed*.

| The spiny oak-gall | The pointed bullet-gall on oak twigs | A cluster of galls on midrib of oak leaf | The acorn plum-gall |

The Gall-Dwellers

He retired to his chamber, took his lamp, and summoned the genius as usual. "Genius," said he, "build me a palace near the sultan's, fit for the reception of my spouse, the princess; but instead of stone, let the walls be formed of massy gold and silver, laid in alternate rows; and let the interstices be enriched with diamonds and emeralds. The palace must have a delightful garden, planted with aromatic shrubs and plants, bearing the most delicious fruits and beautiful flowers. But, in particular, let there be an immense treasure of gold and silver coin. The palace, moreover, must be well provided with offices, storehouses, and stables full of the finest horses, and attended by equerries, grooms, and hunting equipage." By the dawn of the ensuing morning, the genius presented himself to Aladdin, and said, "Sir, your palace is finished; come and see if it accords with your wishes."

—Arabian Nights Entertainments.

ALTHOUGH Aladdin is out of fashion, we still have houses of magic that are even more wonderful than that produced by his resourceful lamp. These houses are built through an occult partnership between insects and plant tissues; and no one understands just how they are made, although we are beginning to understand a little concerning the reasons for the growth. These houses are called galls and are thus well named, since they grow because of an irritation to the plant caused by the insect.

There are many forms of these gall-dwellings, and they may grow upon the root, branch, leaf, blossom, or fruit. The miraculous thing about them is that each kind of insect builds its magical house on a certain part of a certain species of tree or plant; and the house is always of a certain definite form on the outside and of a certain particular pattern within. Many widely differing species of insects are gall-makers; and he who is skilled in gall lore knows, when he looks at the outside of the house, just what insect dwells within it.

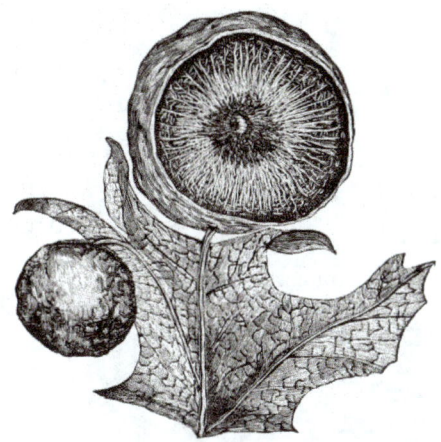

Oak apple, showing the larva of the gall insect

BOB EMBLETON (CC BY-SA 2.0)
Oak apple

We may take the history of the common oak apple, as an example. A little, four-winged, fly-like creature lays its eggs, early in the season, on the leaf of the scarlet oak. As soon as the larva hatches, it begins to eat into the substance of one of the leaf veins. As it eats,

Pineapple gall on a sitka spruce

SAHARADESERTFOX (CC BY-SA 3.0)
Oak artichoke gall

BEATRIZ MOISSET (CC BY-SA 4.0)
Goldenrod round gall

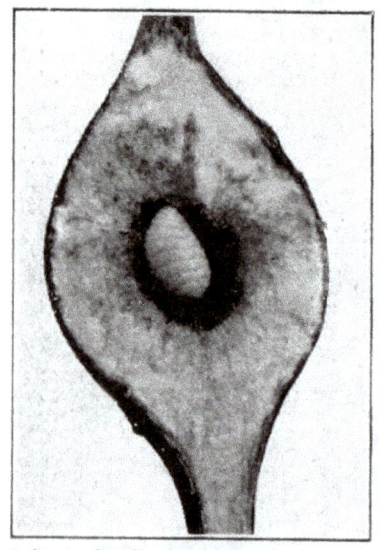

Spherical gall of goldenrod, opened, showing its properous looking owner.

it discharges through its mouth into the tissues of the leaf, a substance which is secreted from glands within its body. Immediately the building of the house commences; out around the little creature grow radiating vegetable fibers, showing by their position plainly that the grub is the center of all of this new growth; meanwhile, a smooth, thin covering completely encloses the globular house; larger and larger grows the house until we are accustomed to call it an oak apple, so large is it. The little chap inside is surely content and happy, for it is protected from the sight of all of its enemies, and it finds the walls of its house the best of food. It is comparable to a boy living in the middle of a giant sponge cake, and who when hungry would naturally eat out a larger cave in the heart of the cake. After the inmate of the oak apple completes its growth, it changes to a pupa and finally comes out into the world a tiny four-winged fly, scarcely a quarter of an inch in length.

The story of the willow cone-gall is quite different. A little gnat lays her eggs on the tip of the bud of a twig; as soon as the grub hatches and begins to eat, the growth of the twig is arrested, the leaves are stunted until they are mere scales and are obliged to overlap in rows around the little inmate, thus making for it a cone-shaped house which is very thoroughly shingled. The inhabitant of this gall is a hospitable little fellow, and his house shelters and feeds many other insect guests. He does not pay any attention to them, being a recluse in his own cell, but he civilly allows them to take care of themselves in his domain, and feed upon the walls of his house. He stays in his snug home all winter and comes out in the spring a tiny, two-winged fly.

There are two galls common on the stems of goldenrod. The more numerous is spherical in form and is made by a fat and prosperous looking little grub which later develops into a fly. But

Mossy rose-gall

although it is a fly that makes the globular gall in the stem of goldenrod, the spindle-shaped gall often seen on the same stem has quite another story. A little brown and gray mottled moth, about three-fourths of an inch long, lays her egg on the stem of the young goldenrod. The caterpillar, when it hatches, lives inside the stem, which accommodatingly enlarges into an oblong room. The caterpillar feeds upon the substance of the stem until it attains its growth, and then seems to dimly realize something about its future needs. At least it cuts, with its sharp jaws, a little oval door at the upper end of its house and makes an even bevel by widening the opening toward the outside. It then makes a little plug of debris which completely fills the door; but because of the bevel, no intrusive beetle or ant can

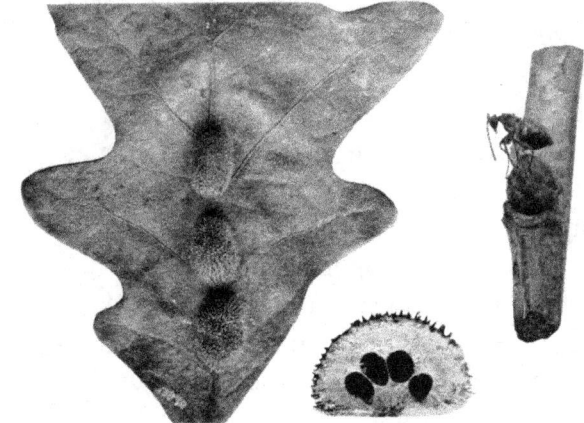

Porcupine gall on leaf of white oak *Section of same showing cells* *Female gall-fly laying eggs in oak bud*

push it in. Thus the caterpillar changes to a helpless pupa in entire safety; and when the little moth issues from the pupa skin, all it has to do is to push its head against the door, and out it falls, and the recluse is now a creature of the outside world.

Many galls are compound, that is, they are made up of a community of larvae, each in its own cell. The mossy rose-gall is an instance of this. The galls made by mites and aphids are open either below or above the surface of the leaf; the little conical galls on witch-hazel are examples of these. In fact, each gall has its own particular history, which proves a most interesting story if we seek to read it with our own eyes.

Lesson

Leading thought— The galls are protective habitations for the little insects which dwell within them. Each kind of insect makes its own peculiar gall on a certain species of plant, and no one understands just how this is done or why it is so.

Method— Ask the pupils to bring in as many of these galls as possible. Note that some have open doors and some are entirely closed. Cut open a gall and see what sorts of insects are found within it. Place each kind of gall in a tumbler or jar covered with cheesecloth and place where they may be under observation for perhaps several months; note what sort of winged insect comes from each.

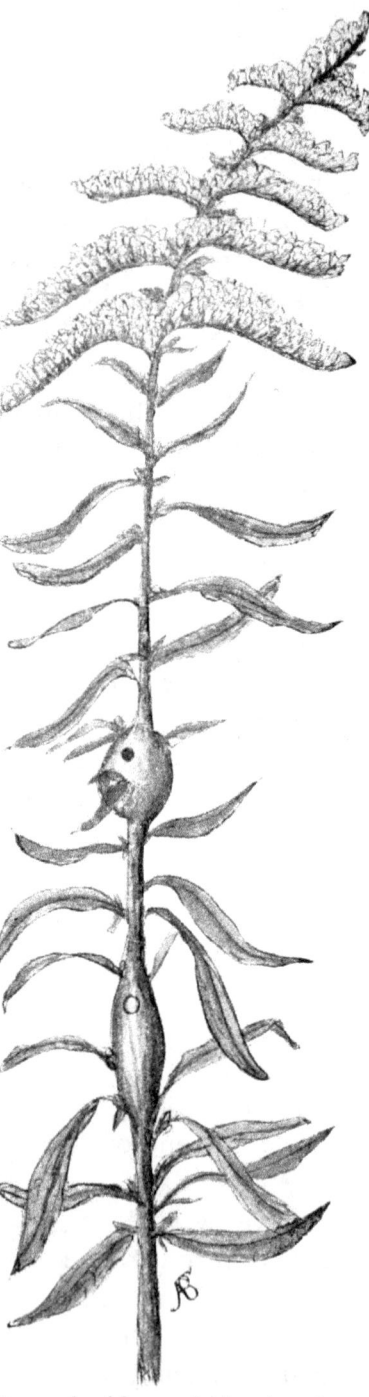

Stem of golden-rod, showing the spherical gall above, made by larva of a fly; and the spindle-shaped gall below, made by the caterpillar of a moth

Rose bedeguar gall on a wild rose (CC BY-SA 3.0)

Observations—

1. On what plant or tree did this gall grow? Were there many like it? Did they grow upon the root, stem, leaf, flower, or fruit? If on the leaf, did they grow upon the petiole or the blade?

2. What is the shape of the little house? What is its color? Its size? Is it smooth or wrinkled on the outside? Is it covered with fuzz or with spines?

3. Open the gall; is there an insect within it? If so, where is it and how does it look? What is the appearance of the inside of the gall?

4. Is there a cell for the insect at the very center of the gall, or are there many such cells?

5. Has the house an open door? If so, does the door open above or below? Are there more than one insect in the galls with open doors? What sort of insect makes this kind of house?

6. Do you find any insects besides the original gall-maker within it? If so, what are they doing?

7. Of what use are these houses to their little inmates? How do they protect them from enemies? How do they furnish them with food?

8. Do the gall insects live all their lives within the galls or do they change to winged insects and come out into the world? If so, how do they get out?

9. How many kinds of galls can you find upon oaks? Upon goldenrod? Upon witch-hazel? Upon willow?

Supplementary reading— Outdoor Studies, Needham, pages 18 and 37; "Houses of Oak," in *Insect Stories*, Kellogg; *Manual for the Study of Insects*.

> *A green little world*
> > *With me at its heart!*
> *A house grown by magic,*
> > *Of a green stem, a part.*
>
> *My walls give me food*
> > *And protect me from foes,*
> *I eat at my leisure,*
> > *In safety repose.*
>
> *My house hath no window,*
> > *'Tis dark as the night!*
> *But I make me a door*
> > *And batten it tight.*
>
> *And when my wings grow*
> > *I throw wide my door;*
> *And to my green castle*
> > *I return nevermore.*

Cola-nut gall

Rosser1954

HTTP://WWW.BIRDPHOTOS.COM (CC BY 3.0)
An american grasshopper

The Grasshopper

Teacher's Story

BECAUSE the grasshopper affords special facilities for the study of insect structure, it has indeed become a burden to the students in the laboratories of American universities. But in nature-study we must not make anything a burden, least of all the grasshopper, which being such a famous jumper as well as flier, does not long voluntarily burden any object.

Since we naturally select the most salient characteristic of a creature to present first to young pupils, we naturally begin this lesson with the peculiarity which makes this insect a "grasshopper." When any creature has unusually strong hind legs, we may be sure it is a jumper, and the grasshopper shows this peculiarity at first glance. The front legs are short, the middle legs a trifle longer, but the femur of the hind leg is nearly as long as the entire body, and contains many powerful muscles which have the appearance of being braided, because of the way they are attached to the skeleton of the leg; the tibia

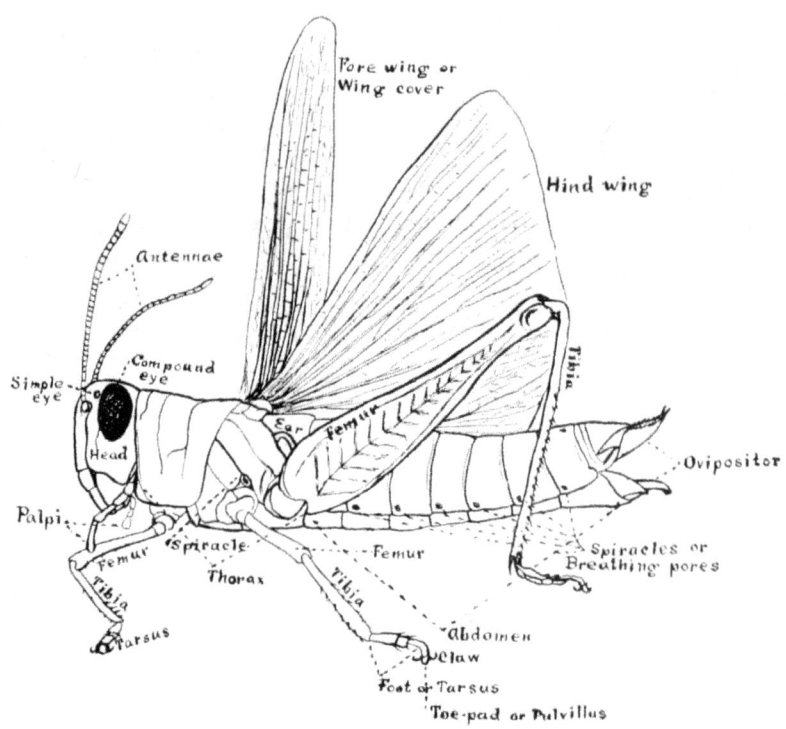
Grasshopper with parts of external anatomy named.

of the hind leg is long and as stiff as if made of steel. When getting ready to jump the grasshopper lowers the great femur below the level of the closed wings and until the tibia is parallel with it and the entire foot is pressed against the ground. The pair of double spines at the end of the tibia, just back of the foot, are pressed against the ground like a spiked heel, and the whole attitude of the insect is tense. Then, like a steel spring, the long legs straighten and the insect is propelled high into the air and far away. This is a remarkable example of insect dynamics; and since so many species of birds feed upon the grasshopper, its leaping power is much needed to escape them. However, when the grasshopper makes a journey it uses its wings.

As we watch a grasshopper crawling up the side of a vial or tumbler we can examine its feet with a lens. Between and in front of the claws is an oval pad which clings to the glass, not by air pressure as was once supposed, but by means of microscopic hairs, called tenent hairs, which secrete a sticky fluid. Each foot consists of three seg-

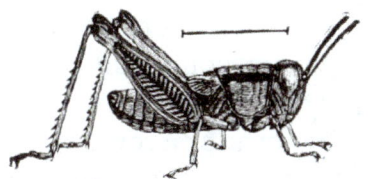
The nymph of the red-legged grasshopper, enlarged.

Adult of red-legged grasshopper

ments and a claw; when the insect is quiet, the entire foot rests upon the ground; but when climbing on glass, the toe pads are used.

The grasshopper's face has a droll expression; would that some caricaturist could analyze it! It is a long face, and the compound eyes placed high upon it, give a look of solemnity. The simple eyes can be made out with a lens. There is one just in front of each big eye, and another, like the naughty little girl's curl, is "right in the middle of the forehead." The antennae are short but alert. The two pairs of palpi connected with the mouth-parts are easily seen, likewise the two pairs of jaws, the notched mandibles looking like a pair of nippers. We can see these jaws much better when the insect is eating, which act is done methodically. First, it begins at one edge of a leaf, which it seizes between the front feet so as to hold it firm; it eats by reaching up and cutting downwards, making an even-edged, long hole on the leaf margin; the hole is made deeper by repeating the process. It sometimes makes a hole in the middle of a leaf and bites in any direction, but it prefers to move the jaws downward. While it is feeding, its palpi tap the leaf continually and its whole attitude is one of deep satisfaction. There is an uprolled expression to the compound eyes which reminds us of the way a child looks over the upper edge of its cup while drinking milk. The grasshopper has a preference for tender herbage, but in time of drouth will eat almost any living plant.

CRISCO 1942 (CC BY-SA 4.0)
Grasshopper infested by mites

Female grasshopper (larger) laying eggs with male in attendance
Http://www.birdphotos.com

Back of the head is a sun-bonnet-shaped piece, bent down at the sides, forming a cover for the thorax. The grasshopper has excellent wings, as efficient as its legs; the upper pair are merely strong, thick, membranous covers, bending down at the sides so as to protect the under wings; these wing-covers are not meant for flying and are held stiff and straight up in the air, during flight. The true wings, when the grasshopper is at rest, are folded lengthwise like a fan beneath the wing-covers; they are strongly veined and circular in shape, giving much surface for beating the air. The grasshoppers' flight is usually swift and short; but in years of famine they fly high in the air and for long distances, a fact recorded in the Bible regarding the plague of locusts. When they thus appear in vast hordes, they destroy all the vegetation in the region where they settle.

The wings of grasshoppers vary in color, those of the red-legged species being gray, while those of the Carolina locusts are black with yellow edges. The abdomen is segmented, as in all insects, and along the lower side there are two lengthwise sutures or creases which open and shut bellows-like, when the grasshopper breathes. The spiracles or breathing pores can be seen on each segment, just above this suture.

The grasshopper has its ears well protected; to find them, we must lift the wings in order to see the two large sounding disks, one on each side of the first segment of the abdomen. These are larger and much more like ears than are the little ears in the elbows of the katydids.

Grasshopper cleaning its antenna

The singing of the short-horned grasshoppers is a varied performance, each species doing it in its own way. One species makes a most seductive little note by placing the femur and tibia of the hind legs together, and with the hind feet completely off the ground, the legs are moved up and down with great rapidity, giving off a little purr. The wings in this case, do not lift at all. There are other species that make the sound by rubbing the legs against the wing-covers.

The grasshopper makes its toilet thus: It cleans first the hind feet by rubbing them together and also by reaching back and scrubbing them with the middle feet; the big hind femur it polishes with the bent elbow of the second pair of legs. It cleans the middle feet by nibbling and licking them, bending the head far beneath the body in order to do it. It polishes its eyes and face with the front feet, stopping to lick them clean between whiles, and it has a most comical manner of cleaning its antennae; this is accomplished by tipping the head sidewise, and bending it down so that the antenna of one side rests upon the floor; it then plants the front foot of that side firmly upon the antenna and pulls it slowly backward between the foot and floor.

The grasshopper has some means of defence as well as of escape; it can give a painful nip with its mandibles; and when seized, it emits copiously from the mouth a brownish liquid which is acrid and ill-smelling. This performance interests children, who are wont to seize the insect by its jumping legs and hold it up, commanding it to "chew tobacco."

Grasshoppers are insects with incomplete metamorphosis, which merely means that the baby grasshopper, as soon as it emerges from the egg, is similar in form to its parent except that it has a very large head and a funny little body, and that it has no quiet stage during life. When immature, the under wings or true wings have a position outside of the wing-covers and look like little fans.

The short-horned grasshoppers lay their eggs in oval masses protected by a tough overcoat. The ovipositor of the mother grasshopper is a very efficient tool, and with it she makes a deep hole in the ground, or sometimes in fence rails or other decaying wood; after placing her eggs in such a cavity, she covers the hiding place with a gummy substance so that no intruders or robbers may work harm to her progeny. Most species of grasshoppers pass the winter in the egg stage; but sometimes we find in early spring the young ones which hatched

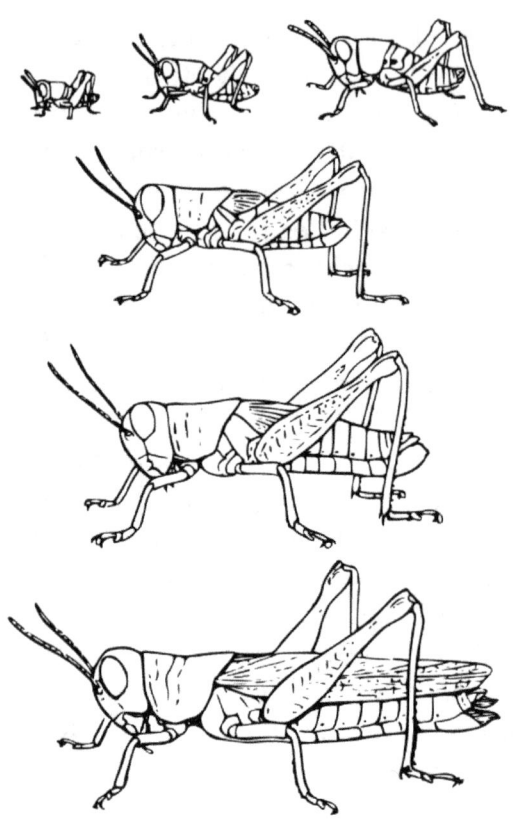

The six stages of development from the newly-hatched nymph to the fully-winged adult grasshopper

in the fall, and they seem as spry as if they had not been frozen stiff.

Lesson

Leading thought— The grasshopper feeds upon grass and other herbage and is especially fitted for living in grassy fields. Its color protects it from being seen by its enemies the birds. If attacked, it escapes by long jumps and by flight. It can make long journeys on the wing.

Method— The red-legged grasshopper (*M. femur-rubrum*) has been selected for this lesson because it is the most common of all grasshoppers, though other species may be used as well. The red-legged locust, or grasshopper has, as is indicated by its name, the large femur of the hind legs reddish in color. Place the grasshopper under a tumbler and upon a spray of fresh herbage, and allow the pupils to observe it at leisure. It might be well to keep some of the grasshoppers in a cage similar to that described for crickets. When studying the feet, or other parts of the insect requiring close scrutiny, the grasshopper should be placed in a vial so that it may be passed around and observed with a lens. Give the questions a few at a time, and encourage the pupils to study these insects in the field.

Observations—

1. Since a grasshopper is such a high jumper, discover if you can how he does this "event." Which pair of legs is the longest? Which

the shortest? How long are the femur and tibia of the hind leg compared with the body? What do you think gives the braided appearance to the surface of the hind femur? What is there peculiar about the hind femur? Note the spines at the end of the tibia just behind the foot.

2. Watch the grasshopper prepare to jump and describe the process. How do you think it manages to throw itself so far? If a man were as good a jumper as a grasshopper in comparison to his size, he could jump 300 feet high or 500 feet in distance. Why do you think the grasshopper needs to jump so far?

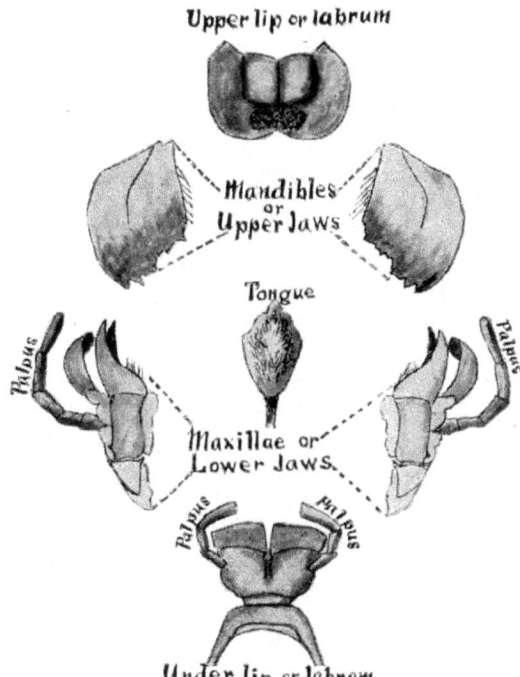

The mouth-parts of a grasshopper dissected off, enlarged and named

3. As the grasshopper climbs up the side of a tumbler or vial, look at its feet through a lens and describe them. How many segments are there? Describe the claws. How does it cling to the glass? Describe the little pad between the claws.

4. Look the grasshopper in the face. Where are the compound eyes situated? Can you see the tiny simple eyes like mere dots? How many are there? Where are they? How long are the antennae? For what are they used?

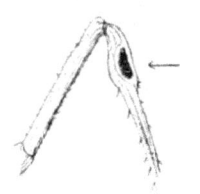

Front leg of katydid, showing ear near elbow

5. How does a grasshopper eat? Do the jaws move up and down or sidewise? What does the grasshopper eat? How many pairs of palpi can you see connected with the mouth-parts? How are these used when the insect is eating? When there are many grasshoppers, what happens to the crops?

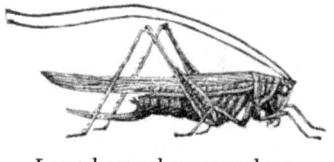
Long horned, or meadow, grasshopper

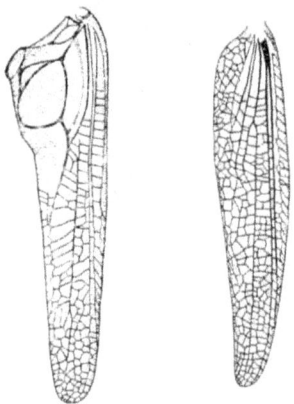
Wing of male and of female meadow grasshoppers

Short-horned and long-horned, or meadow, grasshoppers

6. What do you see just back of the grasshopper's head, when looked at from above?

7. Can the grasshopper fly as well as jump? How many pairs of wings has it? Does it use the first pair of wings to fly with? How does it hold them when flying? Where is the lower or hind pair of wings when the grasshopper is walking? How do they differ in shape from the front wings?

8. Note the abdomen. It is made of many rings or segments. Are these rings continuous around the entire body? Where do their breaks occur? Describe the movement of the abdomen as the insect breathes. Can you see the spiracles or breathing pores? Lift the wings, and find the ear on the first segment of the abdomen.

9. If you seize the grasshopper how does it show that it is offended?

10. How does the grasshopper perform its toilet? Describe how it cleans its antennae, face and legs.

11. What becomes of the grasshoppers in the winter? Where are the eggs laid? How can you tell a young from a full-grown grasshopper?

12. Do all grasshoppers have antennae shorter than half the length of their bodies? Do some have antennae longer than their bodies? Where are the long-horned grasshoppers found? Describe how they resemble the katydids in the way they make music and in the position of their ears.

Supplementary reading— Chapters XVI-XVIII in *Grasshopper Land*, Morley.

The Katydid

Teacher's Story

*"I love to hear thine earnest voice
Wherever thou art hid,
Thou testy little dogmatist,
Thou pretty katydid,*

*Thou mindest me of gentle folks,
Old gentle folks are they,
Thou say'st an undisputed thing
In such a solemn way."*
—Holmes.

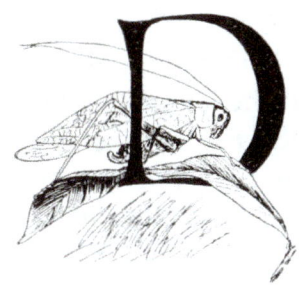

DISTANCE, however, lends enchantment to the song of the katydid, for it grates on our nerves as well as on our ears, when at close quarters. The katydid makes his music in a manner similar to that of the cricket but is not, however, so well equipped since he has only one file and only one scraper for playing. As with the meadow grasshoppers and crickets, only the males make the music, the wings of the females being delicate and normally veined at the base. The ears, too, are in the same position as those of the cricket, and may be seen as a black spot in the front elbow. The song is persistent and may last the night long: "Katy did, she didn't she did." James Whitcomb Riley says, "The katydid is rasping at the silence," and the word rasping well describes the note.

The katydids are beautiful insects, with green, finely veined, leaf-like wing-covers under which is a pair of well developed wings, folded like fans; they resemble in form the long-horned grasshoppers. The common northern species *(Cyrtophyllus)* is all green above except for the long, delicate, fawn-colored antennae and the brownish fiddle of the male, which consists of a flat triangle just back of the thorax where the wing-covers overlap. Sometimes this region is pale brown and sometimes green, and with the unaided eye we can plainly see the strong cross-vein, bearing the file. The green eyes have darker centers and are not so large as the eyes of the grasshopper. The body is green with white lines below on either side. There is a suture the length of the abdomen in which are placed the spiracles. The insect breathes by sidewise expansion and contraction, and the sutures rhythmically open and shut; when they are open, the spiracles can be seen as black dots. The legs are slender and the hind pair, very long. The feet are provided with two little pads, one on each side of the base of the claw. In the grasshopper there is only one pad which is placed between the two hooks of the claw. The female has a green, sickle-shaped ovipositor at the end of the body. With this she lays her flat, oval eggs, slightly over-lapping in a neat row.

Seph (CC BY-SA 3.0)

Katydid eggs attached in rows to a plant stem

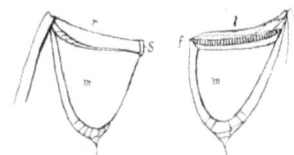

The front portions of the wings of a male katydid showing file on one wing and scraper on the other.

Didier Descouens (CC BY-SA 4.0)

The katydids are almost all dwellers in trees and shrubs; although I have often found our common species upon asters and similar high weeds. The leaf-like wings of these insects are, in form and color, so similar to the leaves that they are very completely hidden. The katydid is rarely discovered except by accident; although when one is singing, it may be approached and ferreted out with the aid of a lantern.

The katydid, when feeding, often holds the leaf or the flower firmly with the front feet, while biting it off like a grazing cow, and if it is tough, chews it industriously with the sidewise working jaws. A katydid will often remain quiet a long time with one long antenna directed forward and the other backward, as if on the lookout for news from the front and the rear. But when the katydid "cleans up," it does a thorough job. It nibbles its front feet, paying special attention to the pads, meanwhile holding the foot to its mandibles with the aid of the palpi. But once washing is not enough; I have seen a katydid go over the same foot a dozen times in succession, beginning always with the hind spurs of the tibia and nibbling along the tarsus to the claws. It cleans its face with its front foot, drawing it downward over the eye and then licking it clean. It cleans its antenna with its mandibles by beginning at the base and drawing it up in a loop as fast as finished. After watching the pro-

The angular-winged katydid and her eggs

cess of these lengthy ablutions, we must conclude that the katydid is among the most fastidious members of the insect "four hundred."

References— *Manual for Study of Insects*, Comstock; *American Insects*, Kellogg; *Ways of Six Footed*, Comstock; *Grasshopper Land*, Morley.

Lesson

Leading thought— The katydids resemble the long-horned grasshoppers and the crickets. They live in trees, and the male sings "katydid" by means of a musical instrument similar to that of the cricket.

Method— Place a katydid in a cricket cage in the schoolroom, giving it fresh leaves or flowers each day, and encouraging the pupils to watch it at recess. It may be placed in a vial and passed around, for close observation. In studying this insect, use the lesson on the red-legged grasshopper and also that on the cricket. These lessons will serve to call the attention of the pupils to the differences and resemblances between the katydid and these two allied insects.

Kevin Judge (CC BY-SA 4.0)

A male fall field cricket

The Black Cricket

Teacher's Story

IF we wish to become acquainted with these charming little troubadours of the field, we should have a cricket cage with a pair of them within it. They are most companionable, and it is interesting to note how quickly they respond to a musical sound. I had a pair in my room at one time, when I lived very near a cathedral. Almost every time that the bells rang during the night, my cricket would respond with a most vivacious and sympathetic chirping.

The patent leather finish to this cricket's clothes is of great use; for, although the cricket is an efficient jumper, it is after all, mostly by running between grass blades that it escapes its enemies. If we try to catch one, we realize how slippery it is, and how efficiently it is thus able to slide through the fingers.

The haunts of the cricket are usually sunny; it digs a little cave beneath a stone or clod in some field, where it can have the whole benefit of all the sunshine, when it issues from its door. These crickets cannot fly, since they have no wings under their wing-covers, as do the grasshoppers. The hind legs have a strong femur, and a short but strong

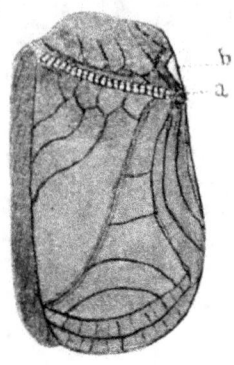

A section of the file enlarged.

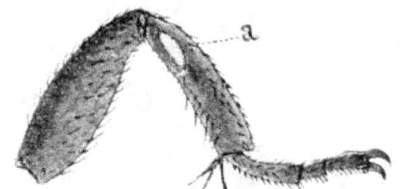

The wing of male cricket enlarged.
a, file b. scraper.

The front leg of a cricket enlarged showing ear at a.

tibia with downward slanting spines along the hind edge, which undoubtedly help the insect in scrambling through the grass. At the end of the tibia, next to the foot, is a rosette of five spines, the two longer ones slanting to meet the foot; these spines give the insect a firm hold, when making ready for its spring. When walking, the cricket places the whole hind foot flat on the ground, but rests only upon the claw and the segment next to it, of the front pairs of feet. The claws have no pads like those of the katydid or grasshopper; the segment of the tarsus next the claw has long spines on the hind feet and shorter spines on the middle and front feet, thus showing that the feet are not made for climbing, but for scrambling along the ground. When getting ready to jump, the cricket crouches so that the tibia and femur of the hind legs are shut together and almost on the ground. The dynamics of the cricket's leap are well worth studying.

The cricket's features are not so easily made out, because the head is polished and black; the eyes are not so polished as the head, and the simple eyes are present but are discerned with difficulty. The antennae are longer than the body and very active; there is a globular segment where they join the face. I have not discovered that the crickets are so fastidious about keeping generally clean as are some other insects, but they are always cleaning their antennas: I have seen a cricket play his wing mandolin lustily and at the same time carefully clean his antenna; he polished these by putting up a foot and bending the antenna down so that his mouth reached it near the base; he then nulled the antenna through his jaws with great deliberation, nibbling it clean to

A female fall field cricket
KEVIN JUDGE (CC BY-SA 4.0)

the very end. The lens reveals to us that the flexibility of the antenna! is due to the fact that they are many jointed. The palpi are easily seen, a large pair above and a smaller pair beneath the "chin." The palpi are used to test food and prove if it be palatable. The crickets are fond of melon or other sweet, juicy fruits, and by putting such food into the cage we can see them bite out pieces with their sidewise working jaws, chewing the toothsome morsel with gusto. They take hold of the substance they are eating with the front feet as if to make sure of it.

The wing-covers of the cricket are bent down at the sides at right angles, like a box cover. The wing-covers are much shorter than the abdomen and beneath them are vestiges of wings, which are never used. The male has larger wing-covers than the female, and they are veined in a peculiar scroll pattern. This veining seems to be a framework for the purpose of making a sounding board of the wing membrane, by stretching it out as a drum-head is stretched. Near the base of the wing-cover, there is a heavy cross-vein covered with transverse ridges, which is called the file; · on the inner edge of the same wing, near the base, is a hardened portion called the scraper. When he makes his cry, the cricket lifts his wing-covers at an angle of forty-five degrees and draws the scraper of the under wing against the file of the overlapping one; lest his musical apparatus become worn out, he can change by putting the other wing-cover above. The wing-covers are excellent sounding boards and they quiver as the note is made, setting the air in vibration, and sending the sound a long distance. The female cricket's wing-covers are more normal in venation; and she may always be distinguished from her spouse by the long sword-like ovipositor at the end of her body; this she thrusts into the ground when she lays her eggs, thus placing them where they will remain safely protected during the winter. Both sexes have a pair of "tail feathers," as the children call them, which are known as the cerci (*sing. cerca*) and are fleshy prongs at the end of the abdomen.

There would be no use of the cricket's playing his mandolin if there were not an appreciative ear to listen to his music. This ear is placed most conveniently in the tibia of the front leg, so that the crickets literally hear with their elbows, as do the katydids and the meadow grasshoppers. The ear is easily seen with the naked eye as a little white, disk-like spot.

The chirp of the cricket is, in literature, usually associated with the coming of autumn; but the careful listener may hear it in early summer, although the song is not then so insistent as later in the season. He usually commences singing in the afternoon and keeps it up periodically all night. I have always been an admirer of the manly, dignified methods of this little "minnesinger," who does not wander abroad to seek his lady love but stands sturdily at his own gate, playing his mandolin the best he is able; he has faith that his sable sweetheart is not far away, and that if she likes his song she will come to him of her own free will. The cricket is ever a lover of warmth and his mandolin gets out of tune soon after the evenings become frosty. He is a jealous musician. When he hears the note of a rival, he at once "bristles up," lifting his wings at a higher angle and giving off a sharp militant note. If the two rivals come in sight of each other, there is a fierce duel. They rush at each other with wide open jaws, and fight until one is conquered and retreats, often minus an antenna, cerca, or even a leg. The cricket's note has a wide range of expression. When waiting for his lady love, he keeps up a constant droning: if he hears his rival, the tone is sharp and defiant; but as the object of his affection approaches, the music changes to a seductive whispering, even having in it an uncertain quiver, as if his feelings were too strong for utterance.

References—*Manual for Study of Insects*, p. 115; *Insect Musicians*; *Ways of the Six Footed*, Comstock.

LESSON

A pair of crickets mating
Kevin Judge (CC BY-SA 4.0)

Leading thought — The crickets are among the most famous of the insect musicians. They live in the fields under stones and in burrows, and feed upon grass and clover. As with the song birds, the male only makes music; he has his wing-covers developed into a mandolin or violin, which he plays to attract his mate and also for his own pleasure.

Method—Make some cricket cages as follows:

Take a small flower-pot and plant in it a root of fresh grass or clover. Place over this and press well into the soil a lantern or lamp chimney. Cover the top with mosquito netting. Place the pot in its saucer, so that it may he watered by keeping the saucer filled. Ask the pupils to collect some crickets. In each cage, place a male and one or more females, the latter being readily distinguished by the long ovipositors. Place the cages in a sunny window, where the pupils may observe them at recess, and ask for the following observations. In studying the cricket closely, it may be well to put one in a vial and pass it around. In observing the crickets eat, it is well to give them a piece of sweet apple or melon rind, as they are very fond of pulpy fruits.

A cricket cage

Observations—

1. Is the covering of the cricket shining, like black patent leather, or is it dull? What portions are dull? Of what use do you think it is to the cricket to be so smoothly polished?

2. Where did you find the crickets? When you tried to catch them, how did they act?

Did they fly like grasshoppers or did they run and leap?

3. Look carefully at the cricket's legs. Which is the largest of the three pairs? Of what use are these strong legs? Look carefully at the tibia of the hind leg. Can you see the strong spines at the end, just behind the foot or tarsus? Watch the cricket jump and see if you can discover the use of these spines. How many joints in the tarsus? Has the cricket a pad like the grasshopper's between its claws? When the cricket walks or jumps does it walk on all the tarsus of each pair of legs?

4. Study the cricket's head. Can you see the eyes? Describe the antenna—their color, length, and the way they are used. Watch the cricket clean its antennae and describe the process. Can you see the little feelers, or pa pi, connected with the mouth? How many are there? How does it use these feelers in tasting food before it eats? Watch the cricket eat, and see whether you can tell whether its mouth is made for biting or sucking.

5. Study the wings. Are the wings of the mother cricket the same size and shape as those of her mate? How do they differ? Does the cricket have any wings under these front wings, as the grasshopper does? Note the cricket when he is playing his wing mandolin to attract his mate. How does he make the noise? Can you see the wings vibrate? Ask your teacher to show you a picture of the musical wings of the cricket, or to show you the wings themselves under the microscope, so that you may see how the music is made.

6. Why does the mother cricket need such a long ovipositor? Where does she put her eggs in the fall to keep them safe until spring?

A pair of dusky lovers

7. Look in the tibia, or elbow, of the front leg for a little white spot.

What do you suppose this is? Are there any white spots like it on the other legs? Ask your teacher to tell you what this is.

8. Can you find the homes of the crickets in the fields? Do

the black crickets chirp in the day-time or after dark? Do they chirp in cold or windy weather, or only when he sun shines?

Supplementary Reading— *Grasshopper Land*, Morley, Chapter XIX.

CRICKET SONG.

Welcome with thy clicking, cricket!
Clicking songs of sober mirth;
Autumn, stripping field and thicket,
Brings thee to my hearth,
Where thy clicking shrills and quickens,
While the mist of twilight thickens.

No annoy, good-humored cricket,
With thy trills is ever blet;
Spleen of mine, how dost thou trick it
To a calm content?
So, by thicket, hearth, or wicket,
Click thy little lifetime, cricket!

BAYARD TAYLOR.

The Black Crickets

Of the insect musicians the cricket is easily the most popular. Long associated with man, as a companion of the hearth and the field, his song touches ever the chords of human experience. Although we, in America, do not have the house-cricket which English poets praise, yet our field-crickets have a liking for warm corners, and will, if encouraged, take up their abode among our hearthstones. The greatest tribute to the music of the cricket is the wide range of human emotion which it expresses. "As merry as a cricket" is a very old saying and is evidence that the cricket's fiddling has ever chimed with the gay moods of dancers and merrymakers. Again, the cricket's song is made an emblem of peace; and again we hear that the cricket's "plaintive cry" is taken as the harbinger of the sere and dying year. From happiness to utter loneliness is the gamut covered by this sympathetic song. Leigh Hunt found him glad and thus addresses him:

> "And you, little housekeeper who class
> With those who think the candles come too soon,
> Loving the fire, and with your tricksome tune
> Nick the glad, silent moments as they pass."
>
> Ways of the Six-footed.

Snowy tree-cricket on a pair of jeans

The Snowy Tree-Cricket

TEACHER'S STORY

THIS is a slim, ghost-like cricket. It is pale green, almost white in color, and about three-fourths of an inch long. Its long, slender hind legs show that it is a good jumper. Its long antennae, living threads, pale gray in color, join the head with amber globe-like segments. The pale eyes have a darker center and the palpi are very long. The male has the wing-covers shaped and veined like those of the black cricket, but they are not so broad and are whitish and very delicate. The wings beneath are wide, for these crickets can fly. The female has a long, sword-like ovipositor.

The snowy tree-cricket, like its relatives, spends much time at its toilet. It whips the front foot over an antenna and brings the base of the latter to the mandibles with the palpi and then cleans it carefully to the very tip. It washes its face with the front foot, always with a downward movement. If the hind foot becomes entangled in anything it first tries to kick it clean, and then drawing it beneath the body, bends the head so as to reach it with the mandibles and nibbles it clean. The middle foot it also thrusts beneath the body, bringing it forward between the front legs for cleaning. But when cleaning its front feet, the snowy tree-cricket puts on airs; it lifts the elbow high and draws the

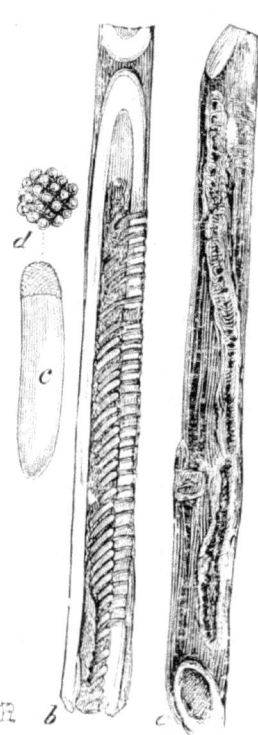

Eggs of snowy tree-cricket, laid in raspberry cane

foot through the mouth with a gesture very like that of a young lady with a seal ring on her little finger, holding the ornate member out from its companions as if it were stiff with a consciousness of its own importance.

There are two common species of the snowy tree-crickets which can hardly be separated except by specialists or by watching their habits. One is called "the whistler" and lives on low shrubs or grass; it gives a clear, soft, prolonged, unbroken note. The other is called "the fiddler" and lives on shrubs and in trees and vines. Its note is a pianissimo performance of the katydid's song; it is delightful, rhythmic and sleep-inspiring; it begins in the late afternoon and continues all night until the early, cold hours of the approaching dawn. The vivacity of the music depends upon the temperature, as the notes are given much more rapidly during the hot nights.

"So far as we know, this snowy tree-cricket is the only one of the insect musicians that seems conscious of the fact that he belongs to an orchestra. If you listen on a September evening, you will hear the first player begin; soon another will join, but not in harmony at first. For some time there may be a see-saw of accented and unaccented notes; but after a while the two will be in unison; perhaps not, however, until many more players have joined the concert. When the rhythmical beat is once established it is in as perfect time as if governed by the baton of a Damrosch or a Thomas. The throbbing of the cricket heart of September, it has been fitly named. Sometimes an injudicious player joins the chorus at the wrong beat, but he soon discovers his error and rectifies it. Sometimes, also, late at night, one part of the orchestra in an orchard gets out of time with the ma-

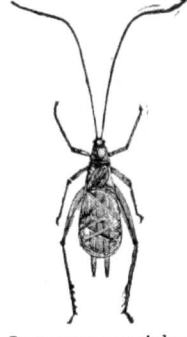

Snowy tree cricket

Snowy tree-cricket

jority, and discord may continue for some moments, as if the players were too cold and too sleepy to pay good attention. This delectable concert begins usually in the late afternoons and continues without ceasing until just before dawn the next morning. Many times I have heard the close of the concert; with the "wee sma'" hours the rhythmic beat becomes slower; toward dawn there is a falling off in the number of players; the beat is still slower, and the notes are hoarse, as if the fiddlers were tired and cold; finally, when only two or three are left the music stops abruptly." *(Ways of the Six-Footed,* Comstock.)

The lesson on this cricket may be adapted from that on the black cricket.

Gary Alpert (cc by 2.5)

The Cockroach

Teacher's Story

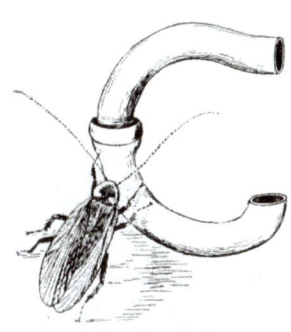

COCKROACHES in our kitchens are undoubtedly an unmitigated nuisance, and yet, as in many other instances when we come to consider the individual cockroach, we find him an interesting fellow and exceedingly well adapted for living in our kitchens despite us.

In shape, the cockroach is flat, and is thus well adapted to slide beneath utensils and into crevices and corners. Its covering is smooth and polished like patent leather, and this makes it slippery and enables it to get into food without becoming clogged by the adherence of any sticky substance. The antennae are very long and flexible and can be bent in any direction. They may be placed far forward to touch things which the insect is approaching, or may be placed over the back in order to be out of the way. They are like graceful, living threads, and the cockroach tests its whole environment with their aid. The mouth has two pairs of palpi or feelers, one of which is very long and noticeable; these are kept in constant motion as if to test the appetizing qualities of food. The

Croton bug

mouth-parts are provided with jaws for biting and, like all insect jaws, these work sidewise instead of up and down. The eyes are black but not prominent or large, and seem to be merely a part of the sleek, polished head-covering.

Some species of cockroaches have wings, and some do not. Those which have wings, have the upper pair thickened and used for wing-covers. The under pair are thinner and are laid in plaits like a fan. The wing-covers are as polished as the body and quite as successful in shedding dirt.

The legs are armed with long spines which are very noticeable and might prove to be a disadvantage in accumulating filth; but they are polished also; and too, this insect spends much time at its toilet.

Cockroaches run "like a streak", children say; so speedily, indeed, do they go that they escape our notice, although we may be looking directly at them. This celerity in vanishing, saves many a cockroach from being crushed by an avenging foot.

When making its toilet, the cockroach draws its long antenna through its jaws as if it were a whiplash, beginning at the base and finishing at the tip. It cleans each leg by beginning near the body and so stroking downward the long spines which seem to shut against the leg. It nibbles its feet clean to the very claws, and scrubs its head vigorously with the front femur.

The cockroach's eggs are laid in a mass enclosed in a pod-shaped covering, which

Preiselbeere (cc by-sa 2.0)
The underside of cockroach

Egg-case of cockroach

is waterproof and polished and protects its contents from dampness. When the cockroaches, or the croton bugs, as the small introduced species of cockroach is called, once become established in a house, the only way to get rid of them is to fumigate the kitchen with carbon bisulphide which is a dangerous performance and should be done only by an expert.

Lesson

Leading thought— The cockroach is adapted for living in crevices, and although its haunts may be anything but clean, the cockroach keeps itself quite clean. The American species live in fields and woods and under stones and sticks and only occasionally venture into dwellings. The species that infest our kitchens and water-pipes are European.

Method— Place a cockroach in a vial with bread, potato or some other food, cork the vial, and pass it around so that the children may observe the prisoner at their leisure.

Observations—

1. What is the general shape of the cockroach? Why is this an advantage? What is the texture of its covering? Why is this an advantage?

2. Describe the antennae and the way they are used. Note the two little pairs of feelers at the mouth. If possible, see how they are used when the cockroach is inspecting something to eat. Can you see whether its mouth is fitted for biting, lapping or sucking its food?

3. Note the eyes. Are they as large and prominent as those of the bees or butterflies?

4. Has this cockroach wings? If so, how many and what are they like? Note two little organs at the end of the body. These are the cerci, like those of the crickets.

5. Describe the general appearance of the cockroach's legs, and tell what you think about its ability as a runner.

6. Note how the cockroach cleans itself and how completely and carefully this act is performed. Have you ever seen cockroach's eggs? If so, describe them.

7. How can you get rid of cockroaches if they invade your kitchen?

LESSON - HOW TO MAKE AN AQUARIUM

THE schoolroom aquarium may be a very simple affair and still be effective. Almost any glass receptacle will do, glass being chosen because of its transparency, so that the life within may be observed. Tumblers, jelly tumblers, fruit jars, butter jars, candy jars and battery jars are all available for aquaria. The tumblers are especially recommended for observing the habits of aquatic insects.

To make an aquarium:

1. Place in the jar a layer of sand an inch or more in depth.
2. In this sand plant the water plants which you find growing under water in a pond or stream; the plants most available are Waterweed, Bladderwort, Water Starwort, Watercress, Stoneworts, Frogspittle or Water-silk.
3. Place on top a layer of small stones or gravel; this is to hold the plants in place.
4. Tip the jar a little and pour in very gently at one side water taken from a pond or stream. Fill the jar to within two or three inches of the top; if it be a jelly tumbler, fill to within an inch of the top.
5. Let it settle.
6. Place it in a window which does not get too direct sunlight. A north window is the best place; if there is no north window to the school room, place it far enough at one side of some other window so that it will not receive too much sunlight.
7. To get living creatures for the aquarium use a dip-net, which is made like a shallow, insect net.
8. Dip deep into the edges of the pond and be sure to bring up some of the leaves and mud, for it is in these that the little water animals live.
9. As fast as dipped up, these should be placed in a pail of water, so that they may be carried to the schoolroom.
10. In introducing the water animals into the aquarium it is well to put but a few in each jar.

The care of the aquarium— Care should be taken to preserve the plant life in the aquarium, as the plants are necessary to the life of the ani-

A humble, but useful, aquarium *An inexpensive and durable aquarium*

mals. They not only supply the food, but they give off oxygen which the animals need for breathing, and they also take up from the water the poisonous carbonic acid gas given off from the bodies of the animals.

1. The aquarium should be kept where there is a free circulation of air.

2. If necessary to cover the aquarium to prevent the insects, like the water boatmen and water beetles, from escaping, tie over it a bit of mosquito netting, or lay upon the top a little square of wire netting used for window screens.

3. The temperature should be kept rather cool; it is better that the water of the aquarium should not be warmer than 50 deg. Fahrenheit, but this is not always possible in the schoolroom.

4. If any insects or animals die in the aquarium they should be removed at once, as the decomposing bodies render the water foul.

5. To feed the animals that live upon other animals take a bit of raw beef, tie a string to it and drop it in, leaving the free end of the string

SPUTNIKTILT (CC BY-SA 3.0)
Side view of a cockroach

outside of the jar. After it has been in one day, pull it out; for if it remains longer it will make the water foul.

6. As the water evaporates it should be replaced with water from the pond.

References— The Fresh Water Aquarium, Eggeling and Ehrenberg; *Insect Life,* Comstock; The Brook Book, Miller; *Nature Study and Life,* Hodge; The Home Aquarium, How to Care for It, Eugene Smith.

BRADLEY RENTZ (CC BY-SA 4.0)
Ants carrying a dead cockroach back to their nest

The Dragon-Flies and Damsel-Flies

TEACHER'S STORY

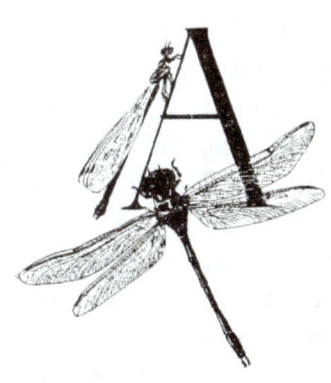

POND without dragon-flies darting above it, or without the exquisitely iridescent damsel-flies clinging to the leaves of its border would be a lonely place indeed. As one watches these beautiful insects, one wonders at the absurd errors which have crept into popular credence about them. Who could be so silly as to believe that they could sew up ears or that they could bring dead snakes to life! The queer names of these insects illustrate the prejudices of the ignorant—devil's darning needles, snake doctors, snake feeders, etc. Despite all this slander, the dragon-flies remain not only entirely harmless to man, but in reality are his friends and allies in waging war against flies and mosquitoes; they are especially valuable in battling mosquitoes since the nymphs, or young, of the dragon-fly, take the wrigglers in the water, and the adults, on swiftest wings, take the mosquitoes while hovering over ponds laying their eggs.

The poets have been lavish in their attention to these interesting insects and have paid them delightful tributes. Riley says:

*"Till the dragon fly, in light gauzy armor burnished bright,
Came tilting down the waters in a wild, bewildered flight."*

Dustin Iskandar (cc by-sa 2.0)
The eyes of a dragon-fly

While Tennyson drew inspiration for one of his most beautiful poems from the two stages of dragon-fly life. But perhaps Lowell in that exquisite poem, "The Fountain of Youth," gives us the perfect description of these insects:

*In summer-noon flushes
When all the wood hushes,
Blue dragon-flies knitting
To and fro in the sun,
With sidelong jerk flitting,
Sink down on the rushes.*

*And, motionless sitting,
Hear it bubble and run,
Hear its low inward singing
With level wings swinging
On green tasselled rushes,
To dream in the sun.*

It is while we, ourselves, are dreaming in the sun by the margin of some pond, that these swift children of the air seem but a natural part of the dream. Yet if we waken to note them more closely, we find many things very real to interest us. First, they are truly children of the sun, and if some cloud throws its shadow on the waters for some moments, the dragon-flies disappear as if they wore the invisible cloak of the fairy tale. Only a few of the common species fly alike in shade and sunshine, and early and late. The best known of these is the big, green skimmer, which does not care so much for ponds, but darts over fields and even dashes into our houses, now and then. Probably

A damsel-fly

it is this species which has started all of the dragon-fly slander, for it is full of curiosity, and will hold itself on wings whirring too rapidly to even make a blur, while it examines our faces or inspects the pictures or furniture or other objects which attract it.

Another thing we may note when dreaming by the pond is that the larger species of dragon-flies keep to the higher regions above the water, while the smaller species and the damsel-flies flit near its surface. Well may the smaller species keep below their fierce kindred, otherwise they would surely be utilized to sate their hunger, for these insects are well named dragons, and dragons do not stop to inquire whether their victims are relatives or not. It is when they are resting, that the dragon and damsel-flies reveal their most noticeable differences. The dragon-fly extends both wings as if in flight while it basks in the sun or rests in the shadow. There is a big, white-bodied species called the whitetail which slants its wings forward and down when it rests; but the damsel-flies fold their wings together over the back when resting. The damsel-flies have more brilliantly colored bodies than do the dragon-flies, many of them being iridescent green or coppery; they are more slender and delicate in form. The damsel-fly has eyes which are so placed on the sides of the head as to make it look like a cross on the front of the body fastened to the slender neck, and with an eye at the tip of each arm. There are very many species of dragon and damsel-flies, but they all have the same general habits.

The dragon-fly nymphs are the ogres of the pond or stream. To anyone unused to them and their ways in the aquarium, there is a surprise in store, so ferocious are they in their attacks upon crea-

Jee & Rani Nature Photography (CC BY-SA 4.0)
Dragonflies mating

tures twice their size. The dragon-fly's eggs are laid in the water; in some instances they are simply dropped and sink to the bottom; but in the case of damsel-flies, the mother punctures the stems of aquatic plants and places the eggs within them. The nymph in no wise resembles the parent dragon-fly. It is a dingy little creature, with six queer, spider-like legs and no wings; although there are four little wing-pads extending down its back, which encase the growing wings. It may remain hidden in the rubbish at the bottom of the pond or may cling to water weeds at the sides, for different species have different habits. But in them all we find a most amazing lower lip. This is so large that it covers the lower part of the face like a mask, and when folded back reaches down between the front legs. It is in reality a grappling organ with hooks and spines for holding prey; it is hinged in such a manner that it can be thrust out far beyond the head to seize some insect, unsuspecting of danger. These nymphs move so slowly and look so much like their background, that they are always practically in ambush awaiting their victims.

The breathing of the dragon-fly nymphs is peculiar; there is an enlargement of the rear end of the alimentary canal, in the walls of which tracheae or breathing tubes extend in all directions. The nymph draws water into this cavity and then expels it, thus bathing the tracheae with the air

Dragon-fly nymph

mixed with water and purifying the air within them. Expelling the water so forcibly, propels the nymph ahead, so this act serves as a method of swimming as well as of breathing. Damsel-fly nymphs, on the other hand, have at the rear end of the body, three long, plate-like gills, each ramified with tracheae.

Nymphs grow by shedding the skin as fast as it becomes too small; and when finally ready to emerge, they crawl up on some object out of the water, and molt for the last time, and are thereafter swift creatures of the air.

References— American Insects, Kellogg. Comstock's Manual.

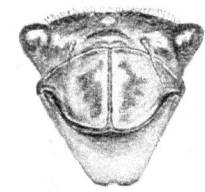

Front view of a dragonfly nymph

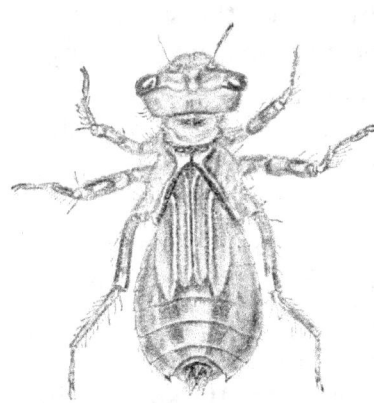

The same nymph seen from above

LESSON

Leading thought— The dragon-flies are among the swiftest of all winged creatures and their rapid, darting flight enables them to hawk their prey, which consists of other flying insects. Their first stages are passed in the bottoms of ponds where they feed voraciously on aquatic creatures. The dragon-flies are beneficial to us because, when very young and when full grown, they feed largely upon mosquitoes.

Method— The work of observing the habits of adult dragon-flies should be largely done in the field during late summer and early autumn. The points for observation should be given the pupils for summer vacation use, and the results placed in the field note-book.

The nymphs may be studied in the spring, when getting material for the aquarium. April and May are the best months for securing them. They are collected by using a dip-net, and are found in the bottoms of reedy ponds or along the edges of slow-flowing streams. These nymphs are so voracious that they cannot be trusted in the aquarium with other insects; each must be kept by itself. They may be fed by placing other water insects in the aquarium with them or by giving them pieces of fresh meat. In the latter case, tie the meat to a thread so that it may be removed after a few hours, if not eaten, since it soon renders the water foul.

The dragon-fly aquarium should have sand at the bottom and some water weeds planted in it, and there should be some object in it which extends above the surface of the water which the nymphs, when ready to change to adults, can climb upon while they are shedding the last nymphal skin, and spreading their new wings.

Loz (CC BY-SA 3.0)
A dragonfly having just shed its nymphal skin

Observations on the young of dragon-flies—

1. Where did you find these insects? Were they at the bottom of the pond or along the edges among the water weeds?

2. Are there any plume-like gills at the end of the body? If so, how many? Are these plate-like gills used for swimming? If there are three of these, which is the longer? Do you know whether the nymphs with these long gills develop into dragon or into damsel-flies?

3. If there are no plume-like gills at the end of the body, how do the insects move? Can they swim? What is the general color of the body? Explain how this color protects them from observation. What enemies does it protect them from?

4. Are the eyes large? Can you see the little wing-pads on the back in which the wings are developing? Are the antennae long?

5. Observe how the nymphs of both dragon and damsel-flies seize their prey. Describe the great lower lip when extended for prey. How does it look when folded up?

6. Can you see how a nymph without the plume-like gills breathes? Notice if the water is drawn into the rear end of the body and then expelled. Does this process help the insect in swimming?

7. When the dragon or damsel-fly nymph has reached its full growth, where does it go to change to the winged form? How does this change take place? Look on the rushes and reeds along the pond margin, and see if you can find the empty nymph skins from which the adults emerged. Where is the opening in them?

Observations on the adult dragon-flies—

1. Catch a dragon-fly, place it under a tumbler and see how it is fitted for life in the air. Which is the widest part of its body? Note the size of the eyes compared with the remainder of the head. Do they almost meet at the top of the head? How far do they extend down the sides of the head? Why does the dragon-fly need such large eyes? Why does a creature with such eyes not need long antennae? Can you see the dragon-fly's antennae? Look with a lens at the little, swollen triangle between the place where the two eyes join and the forehead; can you see the little, simple eyes? Can you see the mouth-parts?

2. Next to the head, which is the widest and strongest part of the body? Why does the thorax need to be so big and strong? Study the wings. How do the hind wings differ in shape from the front wings? How is the thin membrane of the wings made strong? Are the wings spotted or colored? If so, how? Can you see if the wings are folded along the front edges? Does this give strength to the part of the wing which cuts the air? Take a piece of writing paper and see how easily it bends; fold it two or three times like a fan and note how much stiffer it is. Is it this principle which strengthens the dragon-fly's wings? Why do these wings need to be strong?

3. Is the dragon-fly's abdomen as wide as the front part of the body? What help is it to the insect when flying to have such a long abdomen?

Outline for field notes— Go to a pond or sluggish stream when the sun is shining, preferably at midday, and note as far as possible the following things:

Chiswick Chap (cc by-sa 3.0)
Flying in formation

1. Do you see dragon-flies darting over the pond? Describe their flight. They are hunting flies and mosquitoes and other insects on the wing; note how they do it. If the sky becomes cloudy, can you see the dragon-flies hunting? In looking over a pond where there are many dragon-flies darting about, do the larger species fly higher than the smaller ones?

2. Note the way the dragon-flies hold their wings when they are resting. Do they rest with their wings folded together over the abdomen or are they extended out at an angle to the abdomen? Do you know how this difference in attitude of resting determines one difference between the damsel-flies and the dragon-flies?

3. The damsel-flies are those which hold their wings folded above the back when resting. Are these as large and strong-bodied as the dragon-flies? Are their bodies more brilliantly colored? How does the shape of the head and eyes differ from those of the dragon-flies? How many different colored damsel-flies can you find?

4. Do you see some dragon-flies dipping down in the water as they fly? If so, they are laying their eggs. Note if you find others clinging to reeds or other plants with the abdomen thrust below the surface of the water. If so, these are inserting their eggs into the stem of the plant.

Supplementary reading— Outdoor Studies, Needham, p. 54; "The Dragon of Lagunita" in *Insect Stories,* Kellogg.

Bruce Marlin (CC BY-SA 2.5)

The Caddis-Worms and the Caddis-Flies

TEACHER'S STORY

PEOPLE are to be pitied who have never tried to fathom the mysteries of the bottom of brook or pond. Just to lie flat, face downward, and watch for a time all that happens down there in that water world, is far more interesting than witnessing any play ever given at matinee. At first one sees nothing, since all the swift-moving creatures have whisked out of sight, because they have learned to be shy of moving shadows; but soon the crayfish thrusts out his boxing gloves from some crevice, then a school of tiny minnows "stay their wavy bodies 'gainst the stream;" and then something strange happens! A bit of rubbish on the bottom of the brook walks off. Perhaps it is a dream, or we are under the enchantment of the water witches! But no, there goes another, and now a little bundle of sand and pebbles takes unto itself legs. These mysteries can only be solved with a dip-net and a pail half filled with water, in which we may carry home the treasure trove.

When we finally lodge our catch in the aquarium jar, our mysterious moving sticks and stones resolve themselves into little houses built in various fashions, and each containing one inmate. Some of

Ian Alexander (cc by-sa 4.0)
Caddis-fly eggs

the houses are made of sticks fastened together lengthwise; some are built like log cabins, crosswise; some consist simply of a hollow stem cut a convenient length; and some are made of sand and pebbles, and one, the liveliest of all, is a little tube made of bits of rubbish and silk spun in a spiral, making a little cornucopia.

On the whole, the species which live in the log cabins are the most convenient to study. Whatever the shape of the case or house, it has a very tough lining of silk, which is smooth within, and forms the framework to which the sticks and stones are fastened. These little dwellings always have a front door and a back door. Out of the front door may protrude the dark-colored head followed by two dark segments and six perfectly active legs, the front pair being so much shorter than the other two pairs that they look almost like mouth palpi. In time of utter peace, more of the little hermit is thrust out and we see the hind segment of the thorax which is whitish, and behind this the abdomen of nine segments. At the sides of the abdomen, and apparently between the segments, are little tassels of short, white thread-like gills. These are filled with air, impure from contact with the blood, and which exchanges its impurities speedily for the oxygen from the air which is mixed with the water. Water is kept flowing in at the front door of the cabin, over the gills and out at the back door, by the rhythmic movement of the body of the little hermit, and thus a supply of oxygen is steadily maintained.

The caddis-worm is not grown fast to its case as is the snail to its shell. If we hold down with forceps a case in which the occupant is wrong side up, after a few struggles to turn itself over, case and all, it will turn over within the case. It keeps its hold upon the case by two forward-curving hooks, one on each side of the tip of the rear

A caddis-worm removed from its case

segment. These hooks are inserted in the tough silk and hold fast. It also has on top of the first segment of the abdomen a tubercle, which may be extended at will; this helps to brace the larva in its stronghold, and also permits the water to flow freely around the insect. So the little hermit is entrenched in its cell at both ends. When the log-cabin species wishes to swim, it pushes almost its entire body out of the case, thrusts back the head, spreads the legs wide apart, and then doubles up, thus moving through the water spasmodically, in a manner that reminds us of the crayfish's swimming except that the caddis-worm goes head first. This log cabin species can turn its case over dexterously by movements of its legs.

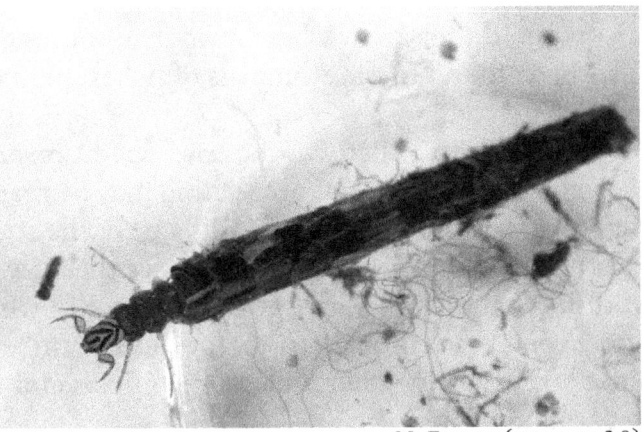

MyForest (cc by-sa 3.0)
Caddis-fly Larva

The front legs of the caddis-worm are so much shorter than the other two pairs that they look like palpi, and their use is to hold close to the jaws bits of food, which are being eaten. The other legs are used for this too if the little legs cannot manage it; perhaps also these short front legs help hold the bits of building material in place while the web is woven to hold it there. The caddis-worm, like the true caterpillars, has the opening of the silk gland near the lower lip. The food of most caddis-worms is vegetable, usually the various species of water plants; but there are some species which are carnivorous, like the net-builder, which is a fisherman.

The caddis-worm case protects its inmate in two ways: First, from the sight of the enemy, and second, from its jaws. A fish comes along and sees a nice white worm and darts after it, only to find a bundle of unappetizing sticks where the worm was. All of the hungry predatory creatures of the pond and stream would be glad to get the caddis-worm, if they knew where it went. Sometimes caddis-worm cases have been found in the stomachs of fishes; perhaps they serve as fish breakfast-food.

While it is difficult to see the exact operation of building the caddis-worm house, the general proceeding may be readily observed. Take a vigorous half-grown larva, tear off part of the sticks and bits of leaves that make the log cabin, and then place the little builder in a tumbler with half an inch of water at the bottom, in which are many bright flower petals cut into strips, fit for caddis lumber. In a few hours the little house will look like a blossom with several rows of bright petals set around its doorway.

When the caddis-worm gets ready to pupate, it fastens its case to some object in the water and then closes its front and back doors. Different species accomplish this in different ways; some spin and fasten a silken covering over the doors; often this is in the form of a pretty grating; others simply fasten the material of which the case is made across the door. But though the door be shut, it is so arranged as to allow the water to flow through and to bring oxygen to the threadlike gills, which are on the pupae as well as on the larvae. When ready to emerge, the pupa crawls out of its case and climbs to some object above the water, sheds its pupa skin, and the adult insect flies off. In some species, living in swift water, the adult issues directly from the water, its wings expanding as soon as touched by the air.

Caddis-flies are familiar to us all even if we do not know them by name. They are night fliers and flame worshippers. Their parchment-like or leathery wings are folded like a roof over the back, and from the side the caddis-fly appears as an elongated triangle with unequal sides. The front wings are long and the hind ones shorter and wider; the antennae are long and threadlike and always waving about for impressions; the eyes are round and beadlike; the tarsi, or feet, are long and these insects have an awkward way of walking on the entire tarsus

A spiral ribbon caddis-worm case. The inmate of this case is a rapid swimmer.

Case and caddis-worm

JAMES K. LINDSEY (CC BY-SA 2.5)
Caddis-fly emerging

which gives them an appearance of kneeling. Most of the species are dull-colored, brownish or gray, the entire insect often being of one color. Caddis-flies would not be so fond of burning themselves in lamps if they had the human sense of smell, for the stench they make when scorching is nauseating. The mother caddis-flies lay their eggs in the water. Perhaps some species drop the eggs in when hovering above, but in some cases the insect must make a diving bell of her wings and go down into the water to place her eggs securely. The wings are covered with hairs and not with scales, and therefore they are better fitted for diving than would be those of the moth. I have seen caddis-flies swim vigorously.

References— *Aquatic Insects*, Miall; *Manual for the Study of Insects*, Comstock.

LESSON

Leading thought— The caddis-worms build around themselves little houses out of bits of sticks, leaves or stones. They crawl about on the bottom of the pond or stream, protected from sight, and able to withdraw into their houses when attacked. The adult of the caddis-worm is a winged moth-like creature which comes in numbers to the light at night.

Method— With a dip-net the caddis-worms may be captured and then may be placed in the school aquarium. Duckweed and other water plants should be kept growing in the aquarium. The log cabin species is best for this study, because it lives in stagnant water and will therefore thrive in an aquarium.

Observations—

1. Where do you find the caddis-worms? Can you see them easily on the bottom of the stream or pond? Why?

Głodny (cc by-sa 3.0)

Waldemartaetz (cc by-sa 4.0)
Caddis-worm cases

2. Of what are the caddis-worm houses made? How many kinds have you ever found? How many kinds of materials can you find on one case? Describe one as exactly as possible. Find an empty case and describe it inside. Why is it so smooth inside? How is it made so smooth? Are all the cases the same size?

3. What does the caddis-worm do when it wishes to walk around? What is the color of the head and the two segments back of it? What is the color of the body? Why is this difference of color between the head and body protective? Is the caddis-worm grown fast to its case, as the turtle is to its shell?

4. Note the legs. Which is the shorter pair? How many pairs? What is the use of the legs so much shorter than the others? If the caddis-worm case happens to be wrong side up, how does it turn over?

5. When it wishes to come to the surface or swim, what does the caddis-worm do? When reaching far out of its case does it ever lose its hold? How does it hold on? Pull the caddis-worm out of its case and see the hooks at the end of the body with which it holds fast.

6. How does the caddis-worm breathe? When it reaches far out of its case, note the breathing gills. Describe them. Can you see how many there are on the segments? How is the blood purified through these gills?

7. What are the caddis-worm's enemies? How does it escape them? Touch one when it is walking, what does it do?

8. On top of the first segment of the abdomen is a tubercle. Do you suppose that this helps to hold the caddis-worm in its case?

9. What does the caddis-worm eat? Describe how it acts when eating.

10. How does the caddis-worm build its case? Watch one when it makes an addition to its case, and describe all that you can see.

11. Can you find any of the cases with the front and back doors closed? How are they closed? Open one and see if there is a pupa

within it. Can you see the growing wings, antennae and legs? Has it breathing filaments like the larva? Cover the aquarium with mosquito netting so as to get all the moths which emerge. See if you can discover how the pupa changes into a caddis-fly.

12. How does the caddis-fly fold its wings? What is the general shape of the insect when seen from the side with wings closed? What is the texture of the wings? How many wings are there? Which pair is the longer?

13. Describe the eyes. The antennae. Does the caddis-fly walk on its toes, or on its complete foot?

14. Examine the moths which come around the lights at night in the spring and summer. Can you tell the caddis-flies from other insects? Do they dash into the light? Do they seem anxious to burn themselves?

Supplementary reading— "A Little Fisherman," *Ways of the Six-Footed*, Comstock.

> *Little brook, so simple so unassuming—and yet how many things love thee!*
> *Lo! Sun and Moon look down and glass themselves in thy waters.*
> *And the trout balances itself hour-long against the stream, watching for its prey; or retires under a stone to rest.*
> *And the water-rats nibble off the willow leaves and carry them below the wave to their nests—or sit on a dry stone to trim their whiskers.*
> *And the May-fly practices for the millionth time the miracle of the resurrection, floating up an ungainly grub from the mud below, and in an instant, in the twinkling of an eye (even from the jaws of the baffled trout) emerging, an aerial fairy with pearl-green wings.*
> *And the caddis-fly from its quaint disguise likewise emerges.*
> *And the prick-eared earth-people, the rabbits, in the stillness of early morning play beside thee undisturbed, while the level sunbeams yet grope through the dewy grass.*
> *And the squirrel on a tree-root—its tail stretched far behind—leans forward to kiss thee,*
> *Little brook, for so many things love thee.*
> —EDWARD CARPENTER.

The Aphids, or Plant-Lice

TEACHER'S STORY

I KNOW of no more diverting occupation than watching a colony of aphids through a lens; these insects are the most helpless and amiable little ninnies in the whole insect world; and they look the part, probably because their eyes, so large and wide apart, seem so innocent and wondering. The usual color of aphids is green. As they feed upon leaves, this color protects them from sight; but there are many species which are otherwise colored, and some have most bizarre and striking ornamentations. In looking along an infested leaf stalk, we see them in all stages and positions. One may have thrust its beak to the hilt in a plant stem, and is so satisfied and absorbed in sucking the juice that its hind feet are lifted high in the air and its antennae curved backward, making altogether a gesture which seems an adequate expression of bliss; another may conclude to seek a new

Perfect bliss!

well, and pulls up its sucking tube, folding it back underneath the body so it will be out of the way, and walks off slowly on its six rather stiff legs; when thus moving, it thrusts the antennae forward, patting its pathway to insure safety. Perhaps this pathway may lead over other aphids which are feeding, but this does not deter the traveler nor turn it aside; over the backs of the obstructionists it crawls, at which the disturbed ones kick the intruder with both hind legs; it is not a vicious kick but a push rather, which says, "This seat reserved, please!"

It is comical to see a row of them sucking a plant stem for "dear life," the heads all in the same direction, and they packed in and around each other as if there were no other plants in the world to give them room, the little ones wedged in between the big ones, until sometimes some of them are obliged to rest their hind legs on the antennae of the neighbors next behind.

Aphids are born for food for other creatures—they are simply little machines for making sap into honey-dew, which they produce from the alimentary canal for the delectation of ants; they are, in fact, merely little animated drops of sap on legs. How helpless they are when attacked by any one of their many enemies! All they do, when they are seized, is to claw the air with their six impotent legs and two antennae, keeping up this performance as long as there is left a leg, and apparently to the very last, never realizing "what is doing." But they are not without means of defence; those two little tubes at the end of the body are not for ornament nor for producing honey-dew for the ants, but for secreting at their tips a globule of waxy substance meant to smear the eyes of the attacking insect. I once saw an aphid perform this act, when confronted by a baby spider; a drop of yellow liquid oozed out of one tube, and the aphid almost stood on its head in order to thrust this offensive globule directly into the face of the spider—the whole performance reminding me of a boy who shakes his clenched fist in his opponent's face and says, "Smell of that!" The spider beat a hasty retreat.

A German scientist, Mr. Busgen, discovered that a plant-louse smeared the eyes and jaws of its enemy, the aphis-lion, with this wax which dried as soon as applied. In action it was something like throwing a basin of paste at the head of the attacking party; the aphis-lion thus treated, was obliged to stop and clean itself before it could go on with its hunt, and the aphid walked off in safety. The aphids surely need this protection because they have two fierce enemies, the larvae of the aphis-lions and of the ladybirds.

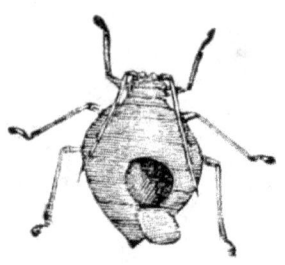

A parasitized aphid enlarged, showing the door cut by the parasite

They are also the victims of parasitic insects; a tiny four-winged "fly" lays an egg within an aphid; the larva hatching from it feeds upon the inner portions of the aphid, causing it to swell as if afflicted with dropsy. Later the aphid dies, and the interloper with malicious impertinence cuts a neat circular door in the poor aphid's skeleton skin and issues from it a full fledged insect.

The aphids are not without their resources to meet the exigencies of their lives in colonies. There are several distinct forms in each species, and they seem to be needed for the general good. During the summer, we find most of the aphids on plants are without wings; these are females which give birth to living young and do not lay eggs. They do this until the plant is overstocked and the food supply seems to be giving out, then another form is produced which has four wings. These fly away to some other plant and start a colony there; but at the approach of cold weather, or if the food plants give out, there are male and female individuals developed, the females being always wingless, and it is their office to lay the eggs which shall last during the long winter months, when the living aphids must die for lack of food plants. The next spring each winter-egg hatches into a female which we call the "stem mother" since she with her descendants will populate the entire plant.

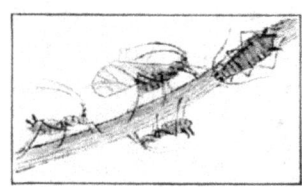

Winged and wingless forms of plant-lice.

Plant-lice vary in their habits. Some live in the ground on the roots of plants and are very destructive; but the greater number of species

live on the foliage of plants and are very fond of the young, tender leaves and thus do great damage. Some aphids have their bodies covered with white powder or with tiny fringes, which give them the appearance of being covered with cotton.

The aphids injuring our flowers and plants may be killed by spraying them with soapsuds made in the proportion of one-quarter pound of ivory soap to one gallon of water. The spraying must be done very thoroughly so as to reach all the aphids hidden on the stems and beneath the leaves. It should be repeated every three days until the aphids are destroyed.

LESSON

Leading thought— Aphids have the mouth in the form of a sucking tube which is thrust into the stems and leaves of plants; through it the plant juices are drawn for nourishment. Aphids are the source of honey-dew of which ants are fond.

Method— Bring into the schoolroom a plant infested with aphids, place the stem in water and let the pupils examine the insects through the lens.

Observations—

1. How are the aphids settled on the leaf? Are their heads in the same direction? What are they doing?

2. Touch one and make it move along. What does it do in order to leave its place? What does it do with its sucking tube as it walks off?

An aphid farming ant sipping some honeydew!

On what part of the plant was it feeding? Why does not Paris green when applied to the leaves of plants kill aphids?

3. Describe an aphid, including its eyes, antennae, legs and tubes upon the back. Does its color protect it from observation?

4. Can you see cast skins of aphids on the plant? Why does an aphid have to shed its skin?

5. Are all the aphids on a plant wingless? When a plant becomes dry are there, after several days, more winged aphids? Why do the aphids need wings?

6. Do you know what honey-dew is? Have you ever seen it upon the leaf? How is honey-dew made by the aphids? Does it come from the tubes on their back? What insects feed upon this honey-dew?

7. What enemies have the aphids?

8. What damage do aphids do to plants? How can you clean plants of plant-lice?

I saw it (an ant), at first, pass, without stopping, some aphids which it did not however disturb. It shortly after stationed itself near one of the smallest, and appeared to caress it, by touching the extremity of its body, alternately with its antennae, with an extremely rapid movement. I saw, with much surprise, the fluid proceed from the body of the aphid, and the ant take it in its mouth. Its antennae were afterwards directed to a much larger aphid than the first, which, on being caressed after the same manner, discharged the nourishing fluid in greater quantity, which the ant immediately swallowed: it then passed to a third which it caressed, like the preceding, by giving it several gentle blows, with the antennae, on the posterior extremity of the body; and the liquid was ejected at the same moment, and the ant lapped it up.

—Pierre Huber, 1810.

Andro96 (cc by-sa 3.0) Jonathan3784 (cc by-sa 3.0)

An ant-lion trap and larva

The Ant-Lion

Teacher's Story

A CHILD is thrilled with fairy stories of ogres in their dens, with the bones of their victims strewn around. The ants have real ogres, but luckily, they do not know about it and so cannot suffer from agonizing fears. The ant ogres seem to have depended upon the fact that the ant is so absorbed in her work that she carries her booty up hill and down dale with small regard for the topography of the country. Thus they build their pits, with instinctive faith that they will some day be entered by these creatures, obsessed by industry and careless of what lies in the path. The pits vary with the size of the ogre at the bottom; there are as many sized pits as are beds in the story of Golden Locks and the bears; often the pits are not more than an inch across, or even less, while others are two inches in diameter. They are always made in sandy or crumbly soil and in a place protected from wind and rain; they vary in depth in proportion to their width, for the slope is always as steep as the soil will stand without slipping.

All that can be seen of the ogre at the bottom, is a pair of long, curved jaws, looking innocent enough at the very center of the pit. If we dig the creature out, we find it a comical looking insect. It is humpbacked, with a big, spindle-shaped abdomen; from its great awkward body projects a flat, sneaking looking head, armed in front with the sickle jaws which are spiny and bristly near the base, and smooth,

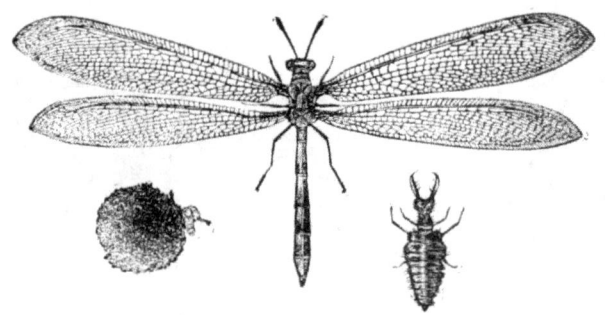
Ant-lion with its cocoon and larva

sharp and curved at the tip. The strange thing about these jaws is that they lead directly to the throat, since the ant-lion has no mouth. Each jaw is made up of two pieces which are grooved where they join and thus form a tube with a hole in the tip through which the industrious blood of the ants can be sucked; not only do the sharp sickle points hold the victim, but there are three teeth along the side of each jaw to help with this. The two front pairs of legs are small and spiny; the hind legs are strong and peculiarly twisted, and have a sharp spikelike claw at the end, which is so arranged as to push the insect backward vigorously if occasion requires; in fact, the ant-lion in walking about, moves more naturally backward than forward because of the peculiar structure of his legs.

Having studied the ogre, we can see better how he manages to trap his victim. As the ant goes scurrying along, she rushes over the edge of the pit and at once begins to slide downward; she is frightened and struggles to get back; just then a jet of sand, aimed well from the bottom of the pit, hits her and knocks her back. She still struggles, and there follows a fusillade of sand jets, each hitting her from above and knocking her down to the fatal center where the sickle jaws await her and are promptly thrust into her; if she is large and still struggles, the big, unwieldy body of the ogre, buried in the sand, anchors him fast and his peculiar, crooked hind legs push his body backward in this strange tug of war; thus, the ant-ogre is not dragged out of his den by the struggles of the ant, and soon the loss of blood weakens her and she shrivels up.

The secret of the jets of sand, lies in the flat head of the ogre; if we look at it regarding it as a shovel, we can see that it is well fitted for its purpose; for it is a shovel with a strong mechanism working it. In fact, the whole pit is dug with this shovel head. Wonderful stories are told about the way that ant-lions dig their pits, marking out the outer margin in a circle, and working inward. However, our common ant-lion of the East simply digs down into the sand and flips the sand out until it makes a pit. If an ant-lion can be caught and put in a jar of sand it will soon make its pit, and the process may be noted carefully.

There is one quality in the ogre which merits praise, and that is his patience.

ENTOMART

An adult ant-lion

There he lies in his hole for days or perhaps weeks, with nothing to eat and no ant coming that way; so when we see an absent-minded ant scrambling over into the pit, let us think of the empty stomach of this patient little engineer which has constructed his pit with such accuracy and so much labor. So precarious is the living picked up by the ant-lions, that it may require one, two or three years to bring one to maturity. At that time it makes a perfectly globular cocoon of silk and sand, the size of a large pea, and within it, changes to a pupa; and when finally ready to emerge, the pupa pushes itself part way out of the cocoon and the skin is shed and left at the cocoon door. The adult resembles a small dragon-fly; it has large net-veined wings and is a most graceful insect, as different as can be from the humpbacked ogre which it once was—a transformation quite as marvelous as that which occurred in Beauty and the Beast. Throughout the Middle West, the ant-lion in its pit is called the "doodle-bug."

Reference— Manual for Study of Insects, Comstock.

LESSON

Leading thought— The ant-lion, or "doodle-bug" makes a little pit in the sand with very steep sides, and hidden at the bottom of it, waits for ants to tumble in to be seized by its waiting jaws. Later the ant-lion changes to a beautiful insect with gauzy wings, resembling a small dragon-fly.

Method— The pupils should see the ant-lion pits in their natural situations, but the insects may be studied in the schoolroom. Some of the ant-lions may be dug out of their pits and placed in a dish of sand. They will soon make their pits, and may be watched during this interesting process. It is hardly advisable to try to rear these insects, as they may require two or three years for development.

Observations—

1. Where were the ant-lion pits out of doors? Were they in a windy place? Were they in a place protected from storms? In what kind of soil were they made?

2. Measure one of the pits. How broad across, and how deep? Are all the pits of the same size? Why?

3. What can you see as you look down into the ant-lion's pit? Roll a tiny pebble in and see what happens. Watch until an ant comes hurrying along and slips into the pit. What happens then? As she struggles to get out how is she knocked back in? What happens to her if she falls to the bottom?

4. Take a trowel and dig out the doodle-bug. What is the shape of its body? What part of the insect did you see at the bottom of the pit? Do you know that these great sickle-shaped jaws are hollow tubes for sucking blood? Does the ant-lion eat anything except the blood of its victim?

5. Can you see that the ant-lion moves backward more easily than forward? How are its hind legs formed to help push it backward? How does this help the ant-lion in holding its prey? How does the big awkward body of the ant-lion help to hold it in place at the bottom of the pit when it seizes an ant in its jaws?

6. What shape is the ant-lion's head? How does it use this head in taking its prey? In digging its pit?

7. Take a doodle-bug to the schoolroom, place it in a dish of sand, covered with glass, and watch it build its pit.

8. Read in the entomological books about the cocoon of the ant-lion and what the adult looks like, and then write an ant-lion autobiography.

Supplementary reading— Insect Stories, Kellogg, "The True Story of Morrowbie Jukes."

Green lacewing   Alvesgaspar (CC BY-SA 4.0)

The Mother Lace-Wing and the Aphis-Lion

Teacher's Story

FLITTING leisurely through the air on her green gauze wings, the lace-wing seems like a filmy leaf, broken loose and drifting on the breeze. But there is purpose in her flight, and through some instinct she is enabled to seek out an aphis-ridden plant or tree, to which she comes as a friend in need. As she alights upon a leaf, she is scarcely discernible because of the pale green of her delicate body and wings; however, her great globular eyes that shine like gold attract the attention of the careful observer. But though she is so fairy-like in appearance, if you pick her up, you will be sorry if your sense of smell is keen, for she exhales a most disagreeable odor when disturbed—a habit which probably protects her from birds or other creatures which might otherwise eat her.

However, if we watch her we shall see that she is a canny creature despite her frivolous appearance; her actions are surely peculiar. A drop of sticky fluid issues from the tip of her body, and she presses it down on the surface of the leaf; then lifting up her slender abdomen like a distaff, she spins the drop into a thread a half inch long or more, which the air soon dries; and this silken thread is stiff enough to sustain an oblong egg, as large as the point of a pin, which she lays at the very tip of it. This done she lays another egg in a like manner, and when she is through, the leaf looks as if it were covered with spore cases of a glittering white mold. This done she flies off and disports herself in the sunshine, care free, knowing that she has done all she can for her family.

After a few days the eggs begin to look dark, and then if we examine them with a lens, we may detect that they contain little doubled-up creatures. The first we see of the egg inmate as it hatches, is a pair of jaws thrust through the shell, opening it for a peep-hole; a little later the owner of the jaws, after resting a while with an eye on the world which he is so soon to enter, pushes out his head and legs and drags out a tiny, long body, very callow-looking and clothed in long, soft hairs. At first the little creature crawls about his egg-shell, clinging tightly with all his six claws, as if fearful of such a dizzy height above his green floor; then he squirms around a little and thrusts out a head inquiringly while still hanging on "for dear life." Finally he gains courage and prospects around until he discovers his egg stalk, and then begins a rope climbing performance, rather difficult for a little chap not more than ten minutes old. He takes a careful hold with his front claws, the two other pairs of legs carefully balancing for a second, and then desperately seizing the stalk with all his clasping claws, and with many new grips and panics, he finally achieves the bottom in safety. As if dazed by his good luck, he stands still for a time, trying to make up his mind what has happened and what to do next; he settles the matter by trotting off to make his first breakfast of aphids; and now we can see that it is a lucky thing for his brothers and sisters, still unhatched, that they are high above his head and out of reach, for he might not be discriminating in the matter of

Aphis-lion, eggs, larva, cocoon and the adult, lace wing.

his breakfast food, never having met any of his family before. He is a queer looking little insect, spindle-shaped and with peculiarly long, sickle-shaped jaws projecting from his head. Each of these jaws is made up of two pieces joined length-wise so as to make a hollow tube, which has an opening at the tip of the jaw, and another one at the base which leads directly to the little lion's throat. Watch him as he catches an aphid; seizing the stupid little bag of sap in his great pincers, he lifts it high in the air, as if drinking a bumper, and sucks its green blood until it shrivels up, kicking a remonstrating leg to the last. It is my conviction that aphids never realize when they are being eaten; they simply dimly wonder what is happening.

Eric Steinert (cc by-sa 3.0)
Lacewing larva feeding on an aphid

It takes a great many aphids to keep an aphis-lion nourished until he gets his growth; he grows like any other insect by shedding his skeleton skin when it becomes too tight. Finally he doubles up and spins around himself a cocoon of glistening white silk, leaving it fastened to the leaf; when it is finished, it looks like a seed pearl, round and polished. I wish some child would watch an aphis-lion weave its cocoon and tell us how it is done! After a time, a week or two perhaps, a round little hole is cut in the cocoon, and there issues from it a lively little green pupa, with wing pads on its back; but he very soon sheds his pupa skin and issues as a beautiful lace-wing fly with golden eyes and large, filmy, iridescent, pale green wings.

Lesson

Leading thought— The lace-wing fly or golden-eyes, as she is called, is the mother of the aphis-lion. She lays her eggs on the top of stiff, silken stalks. The young aphis-lions when hatched, clamber down upon the leaf and feed upon plant-lice, sucking their blood through their tubular jaws.

Method— Through July and until frost, the aphis-lions may be found on almost any plant infested with plant-lice; and the lace-wing's eggs or egg-shells on the long stalks are also readily found. All these may be brought to the schoolroom. Place the stem of a plant infested with aphids in a jar of water, and the acts of the aphis-lions as well as the habits of the aphids may be observed during recess or at other convenient times, by all the pupils.

Observations—

1. When you see a leaf with some white mold upon it, examine it with a lens; the mold is likely to be the eggs of the lace-wing. Is the egg as large as a pin head? What is its shape? What is its color? How long is the stalk on which it is placed? Of what material do you think the stalk is made? Why do you suppose the lace-wing mother lays her eggs on the tips of stalks? Are there any of these eggs near each other on the leaf?

2. If the egg is not empty, observe through a lens how the young aphis-lion breaks its egg-shell and climbs down.

3. Watch an aphis-lion among the plant-lice. How does it act? Do the aphids seem afraid? Does the aphis-lion move rapidly? How does it act when eating an aphid?

4. What is the general shape of the aphis-lion? Describe the jaws. Do you think these jaws are used for chewing, or merely as tubes through which the green blood of the aphids is sucked? Do the aphis-lions ever attack each other or other insects? How does the aphis-lion differ in appearance from the ladybird larva?

5. What happens to the aphis-lion after it gets its growth? Describe its cocoon if you can find one.

6. Describe the little lace-wing fly that comes from the cocoon. Why is she called golden-eyes? Why lace-wing? Does she fly rapidly? Do you suppose that if she should lay her eggs flat on a leaf, that the first aphis-lion that hatched would run about and eat all its little brothers and sisters which were still in their egg-shells? How do the aphis-lions benefit our rose bushes and other cultivated plants?

Supplementary reading— "A Tactful Mother" in *Ways of the Six-Footed*.

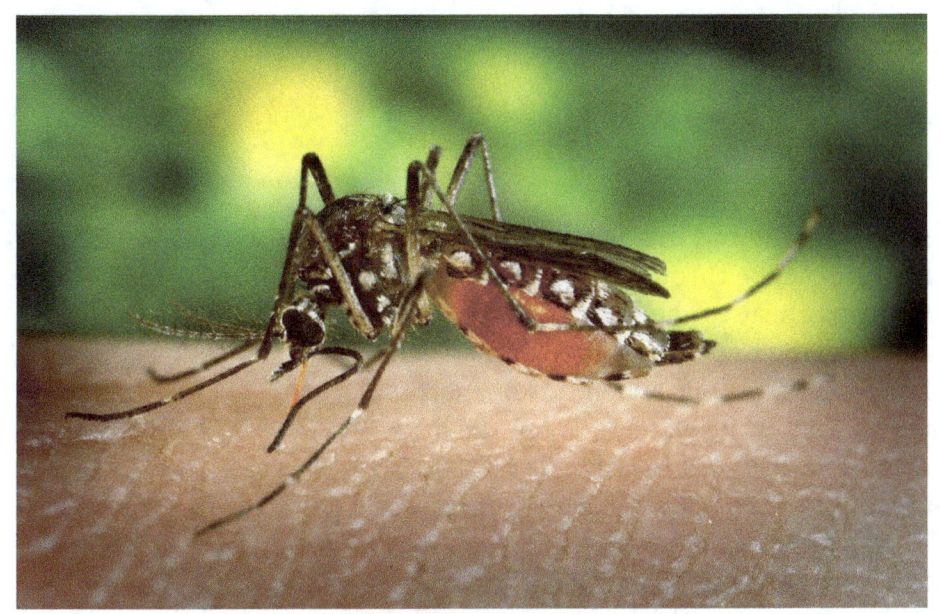

The Mosquito

TEACHER'S STORY

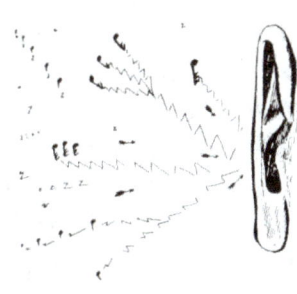

IN DEFIANCE of the adage, the mother of our most common mosquitoes does not hesitate to put her eggs all in one basket, but perhaps she knows it is about the safest little basket for eggs in this world of uncertainties. If it were possible to begin this lesson with the little boat-shaped egg baskets, I should advise it. They may be found in almost any rain barrel, and the eggs look like a lot of tiny cartridges set side by side, points up, and lashed or glued together, so there shall be no spilling. Like a certain famous soap, they "float," coming up as dry as varnished corks when water is poured upon them.

The young mosquito, or wriggler, breaks through the shell of the lower end of the egg and passes down into the water, and from the first, it is a most interesting creature to view through a hand lens. The head and the thorax are rather large while the body is tapering and armed with bunches of hairs. At the rear of the body are two tubes very different in shape; one is long, straight and unadorned; this is the breathing tube through which air passes to the tracheae of the body. This tube has a star-shaped valve at the tip, which can be opened and shut; when it is opened at the surface of the water, it keeps the little creature afloat and meanwhile allows air to pass into the body. When the wriggler is thus hanging at an angle of 45 degrees to the surface of the water, it feeds upon small particles of decaying vegetation; it has a remarkable pair of jaws which are armed with brushes, which in our common species, by moving rapidly, set up currents and bring the food to the mouth. This process can be seen plainly with a lens. When disturbed, the wriggler shuts the valve to its breathing tube, and sinks. However, it is not much heavier than the water; I have often seen one rise for some distance without apparent effort. The other tube at the end of the body, supports the swimming organs, which consist of four finger-like processes and various bunches of hairs. When swimming, the wriggler goes tail first, the swimming organs seeming to take hold of the water and to pull the creature backward, in a series of spasmodic jerks; in fact, the insect seems simply to "throw somersaults," like an acrobat. I have often observed wrigglers standing on

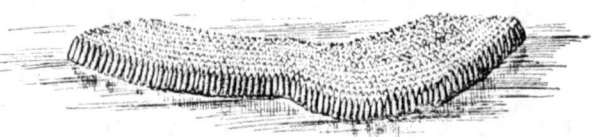

The egg-raft of a mosquito

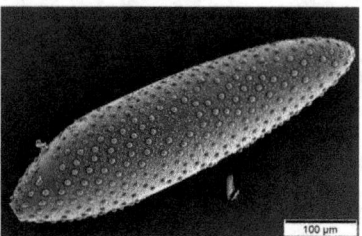

MOGANA DAS MURTEY (CC BY-SA 3.0)
Mosquito egg

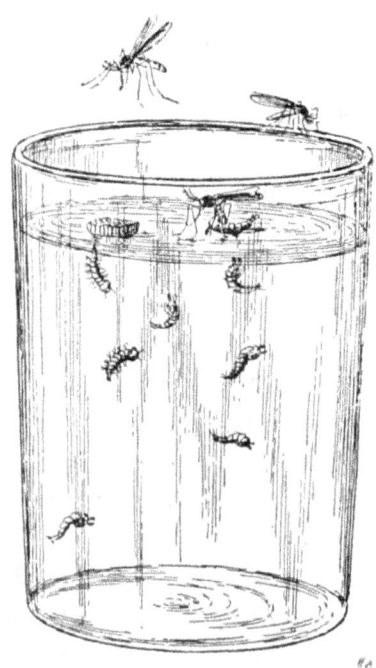

A mosquito aquarium

their heads in the bottom of the aquarium, with their jaws bent under, revolving their brushes briskly; but they never remain very long below the surface, as it is necessary for them to take in fresh air often.

The pupa has the head and thoracic segments much enlarged, making it all "head and shoulders" with a quite insignificant body attached. Upon the thorax are two breathing tubes, which look like two ears, and therefore when the pupa rests at the surface of the water, it remains head up so that these tubes may take in the air; at the end of the body are two swimming organs which are little, leaf-like projections. At this stage the insect is getting ready to live its life in the air, and for this reason probably, the pupa rests for long periods at the surface of the water and does not swim about much, unless disturbed. However, it is a very strange habit for a pupa to move about at all. In the case of other flies, butterflies, and moths, the pupa stage is quiet.

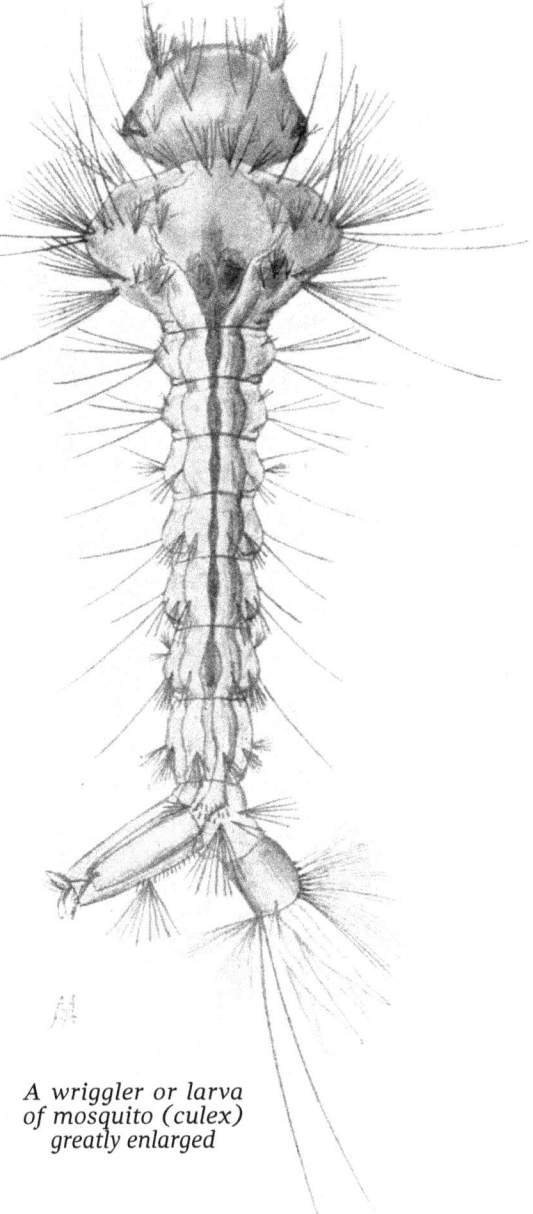

A wriggler or larva of mosquito (culex) greatly enlarged

When fully mature, the pupa rises to the surface of the water, the skeleton skin breaks open down its back and the mosquito carefully works itself out, until its wings are free and dry, meanwhile resting upon the floating pupa skin. This is indeed a frail bark, and if the slightest breeze ruffles the water, the insect is likely to drown before its wings are hard enough for flight.

The reason that kerosene oil, put upon the surface of the water where mosquitoes breed, kills the insects is because both the larvae and pupae of mosquitoes are obliged to rise to the surface, and push their breathing tubes through the surface film so that they will open to the air; a coating of oil on the water prevents this, and they are suffocated. Also when the mosquito emerges from the pupa skin, if it is even touched by the oil, it is unable to fly and soon dies.

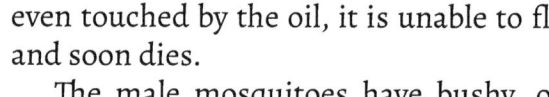

Antenna of male mosquio enlarged

The male mosquitoes have bushy, or feathery, antennae. These antennae are hearing organs of very remarkable construction. The Anopheles may be distinguished from the Culex by the following characteristics: Its wings are spotted instead of plain. When at rest it is perfectly straight, and is likely to have the hind legs in the air. It may also rest at an angle to the surface to which it clings. The Culex is not spotted on the wings and is likely to be humped up when at rest. In our climate the Anopheles is more dangerous than the Culex because it carries the germs of malaria. A mosquito's wing under a microscope is a most beautiful object, as it is "trimmed" with ornamental scales about the edges and along the veins. The male mosquitoes neither sing nor bite; the song of the female mosquito is supposed to be made by the rapid vibration of the wings, and her musical performances are for the purpose of attracting her mate, as it has been shown that he can hear

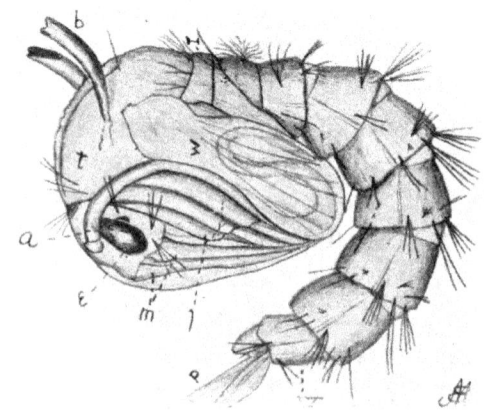

The pupa of a mosquito greatly magnified. Note the breathing tubes near the head

Anopheles mosquitos can transmit malaria

through his antennae a range of notes covering the middle and next higher octaves of the piano.

Of late we are learning that the mosquitoes are in a very strange way a menace to health. Through a heroism, as great as ever shown on field of battle, men have imperiled their lives to prove that the germs of the terrible yellow fever were transmitted by the biting mosquito, and with almost equal bravery other men have demonstrated that the germs of malaria are also thus carried.

In the North, our greatest danger is from the mosquitoes which carry the malarial germs, and these are the mosquitoes with spotted wings and belong to the genus Anopheles. This mosquito, in order to be of danger to us, must first feed upon the blood of some person suffering from malaria (ague) and thus take the germ of the disease into its stomach. Here the germ develops and multiplies into many minute germs, which pass through another stage and finally get into the blood of the mosquito and accumulate in the salivary glands. The reason any mosquito bite or insect bite swells and itches is because, as the insect's beak is inserted into the flesh, it carries with it some of the saliva from the insect's mouth. In the case of Anopheles these malarial germs are carried with the saliva into the blood of the victim. It has been proven

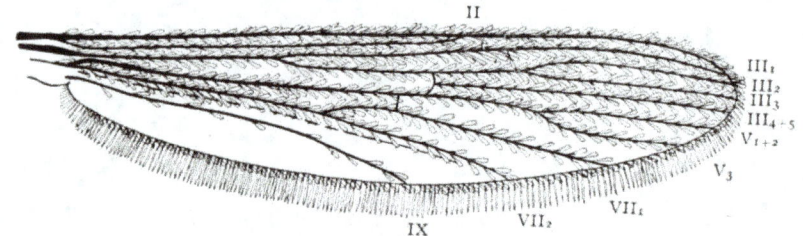
Wing of mosquito enlarged

that in the most malarial countries, like Italy and India, people are entirely free from malaria if they are not bitten by mosquitoes.

After this explanation has been made, it would be well for the teacher to take the pupils on a tour of inspection through the neighborhood to see if there are any mosquito larvae in rain barrels, ponds or pools of stagnant water. If such places are found, let the pupils themselves apply the following remedies:

1. Rain barrels should be securely covered.

2. All stagnant pools should be drained and filled up if possible.

3. Wherever there are ponds or pools where mosquitoes breed that cannot be filled or drained, the surface of the water should be covered with a spray of kerosene oil. This may be applied with a spray pump or from a watering can.

4. If it is impracticable to cover such places with oil, introduce into such pools the following fish: Minnows, sticklebacks, sunfish and goldfish.

GEOFF GALLICE (CC BY-SA 2.0)
Not even the snakes scales can protect it from the mosquito

The effect of this lesson upon the children should be to impress them with the danger to life and health from mosquitoes and to implant in them a determination to rid the premises about their homes of these pests.

References— Farmers' Bulletin No. 155, U. S. Department of Agriculture, by L. O. Howard; leaflet in Reading Course for Farmers' Wives, series 2, No. 10, by M. V. Slingerland; *American Insects*, Kellogg; *The Insect Book*, Howard; *Insect Life, The Manual for the Study of Insects*, Comstock; *Ways of the Six-Footed*, Comstock.

LESSON

Leading thought— The wrigglers, or wigglers, which we find in rain-barrels and stagnant water are the larvae of mosquitoes. We should study their life history carefully if we would know how to get rid of mosquitoes.

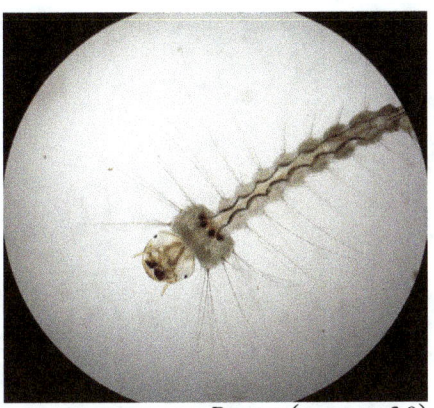

RKITKO (CC BY-SA 3.0)
Note the segmentation and circulatory system

Method— There is no better way to interest the pupils in mosquitoes than to place in an aquarium jar in the schoolroom a family of wrigglers from some pond or rain barrel. For the pupils' personal observation, take some of the wrigglers from the aquarium with a pipette and place them in a homeopathic vial; fill the vial three-fourths full of water and cork it. Pass it around with a hand lens and give each pupil the opportunity to observe it for five or ten minutes. It would be well if this vial could be left on each desk for an hour or so during study periods, so that the observations may be made casually and leisurely. While the pupils are studying the wrigglers, the following questions should be placed upon the blackboard, and each pupil should make notes which may finally be given at a lesson period. This is particularly available work for September.

In studying the adult mosquito, a lens or microscope is necessary. But it is of great importance that the pupils be taught to discriminate between the comparatively harmless species of Culex and the dangerous Anopheles and therefore they should be taught to be observant of the way mosquitoes rest upon the walls, and whether they have mottled or clear wings.

THE LARVA

Observations:

1. Note if all the wrigglers are of the same general shape, or if some of

Larvae of an Anopheles mosquito

them have a very large head; these latter are the pupae and the former are the larvae. We will study the larvae first. Where do they rest when undisturbed? Do they rest head up or down? Is there any part of their body that comes to the surface of the water?

2. When disturbed what do they do? When they swim, do they go head or tail first? When they float do they go upward or downward?

3. Observe one resting at the top. At what angle does it hold itself to the surface of the water? Observe its head. Can you see the jaw brushes revolving rapidly? What is the purpose of this? Describe its eyes. Can you see its antennae?

4. Note the two peculiar tubes at the end of the body and see if you can make out their use.

5. Note especially the tube that is thrust up to the surface of the water when the creatures are resting. Can you see how the opening of this tube helps to keep the wriggler afloat? What do you think is the purpose of this tube? Why does it not become filled with water when the wriggler is swimming? Can you see the two air vessels, or tracheae, extending from this tube along the back the whole length of the body?

6. Note the peculiarities of the other tube at the rear end of the body. Do you think the little finger-like projections are an aid in swimming? How many are there?

7. Can you see the long hairs along the side of the body?

8. Does the mosquito rest at the bottom of the bottle or aquarium?

THE PUPA

9. What is the most noticeable difference in appearance between the larva and pupa?

10. When the pupa rests at the surface of the water, is it the same end up as the wriggler?

11. Note on the "head" of the pupa two little tubes extending up like ears. These are the breathing tubes. Note if these open to the air when the pupa rests at the surface of the water.

12. Can you see the swimming organs at the rear of the body of the pupa? Does the pupa spend a longer time resting at the surface than the larva? How does it act differently from the pupae of other flies and moths and butterflies?

13. How does the mosquito emerge from the pupa skin? Why does kerosene oil poured on the surface of the water kill mosquitoes?

THE ADULT MOSQUITO

1. Has the mosquito feathery antennae extending out in front? If so, what kind of mosquitoes are such?

2. Do the mosquitoes with bushy antennae bite? Do they sing?

3. Are the wings of the mosquito spotted or plain? How many has it?

4. When at rest, is it shortened and humpbacked or does it stand straight out with perhaps its hind legs in the air?

5. What are the characteristics by which you can tell the dangerous Anopheles?

6. Why is the Anopheles more dangerous than the Culex?

7. Examine a mosquito's wing under a microscope and describe it.

8. Examine the antennae of a male and a female mosquito under a microscope, and describe the difference.

9. Which sex of the mosquito does the biting and the singing?

10. How is the singing done?

The House-Fly

TEACHER'S STORY

THE house-fly is surely an up-to-date member of that select class which evolutionists call the "fit." It flourishes in every land, plumping itself down in front of us at table, whether we be eating rice in Hong Kong, dhura in Egypt, macaroni in Italy, pie in America, or tamales in Mexico. There it sits, impertinent and imperturbable, taking its toll, letting down its long elephant-trunk tongue, rasping and sucking up such of our meal as fits its needs. As long as we simply knew it as a thief we, during untold ages, merely slapped it and shooed it, which effort on our part apparently gave it exhilarating exercise. But during recent years we have begun trapping and poisoning, trying to match our brains against its agility; although we slay it by thousands, we seem only to make more room for its well-fed progeny of the future, and in the end we seem to have gained nothing. But the most recent discoveries of science have revealed to us, that what the house-fly takes of our food, is of little consequence to what it leaves behind. Because of this, we have girded up our loins and gone into battle in earnest.

I have always held that nature-study should follow its own peaceful path and not be the slave of economic science. But occasionally it seems necessary, when it is a question of creating public sentiment, and of cultivating public intelligence in combating a great peril, to make nature-study a handmaiden, if not a slave, in this work. If our woods were filled with wolves and bears, as they were in the days of my grandfather, I should give nature-study lessons on these animals, which would lead to their subjugation. Bears and wolves trouble us no more; but now we have enemies far more subtle, in the ever-present microbes, which we may never hope to conquer but which, with proper precautions, we may render comparatively harmless. Thus, our nature-study with insects which carry disease, like the mosquitoes, flies and fleas, must be a reconnaissance for a war of extermination; the fighting tactics may be given in lessons on health and hygiene.

Sanjay Acharya (cc by-sa 4.0)
The eyes and head of a housefly

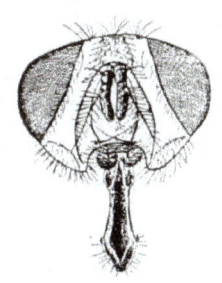
Head of fly showing eyes, antennae and mouth-parts

Perhaps if a fly were less wonderfully made, it would be a less convenient vehicle for microbes. Its eyes are two great, brown spheres on either side of the head, and are composed of thousands of tiny six-sided eyes that give information of what is coming in any direction; in addition, it has on top of the head, looking straight up, three tiny,

Robert D. Anderson (cc by-sa 3.0)
A micrograph of the foot of house-fly

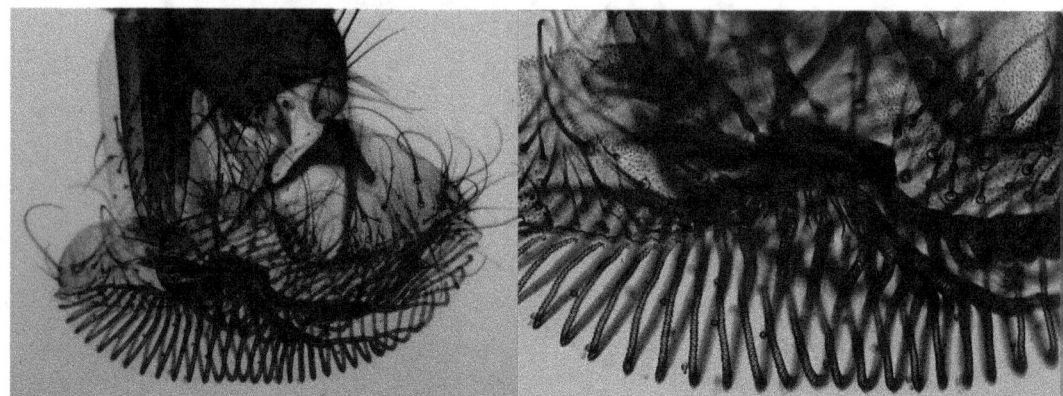

JOHN ALAN ELSON (CC BY-SA 4.0)

A housefly mouth magnified 40x and 100x

shining, simple eyes, which cannot be seen without a lens. Its antennae are peculiar in shape, but are evidently sense organs; it is attracted from afar by certain odors, and so far as we can discover, its antennae are all the nose it has. Its mouth-parts are all combined to make a most amazing and efficient organ for getting food; at the tip are two flaps, which can rasp a substance so as to set free the juices, and above this is a tube, through which the juices may be drawn to the stomach. This tube is extensible, being conveniently jointed so that it can be folded under the "chin" when not in use. This is usually called the fly's tongue, but it is really all the mouth parts combined, as if a boy had his lips, teeth and tongue, standing out from his face, at the end of a tube a foot long.

The thorax can be easily studied; it is striped black and white above and bears the two wings, and the two little flaps that are called balancers and which are probably remnants of hind wings which the remote ancestors of flies flew with. The fly's wing is a transparent but strong membrane strengthened by veins, and is prettily iridescent. The thorax bears on its lower side the three pairs of legs. The abdomen consists of five segments and is covered with stiff hairs. The parts of the leg, seen when the fly is walking, consists of three segments, the last segment or tarsus being more slender, and if looked at with a lens, is seen to be composed of five segments, the last of which bears the claws; it is with these claws that the fly walks, although all of the five segments really form the foot; in other words, it walks on its tip-toes. But it clings to ceilings by means of the two little pads below the claws, which are cov-

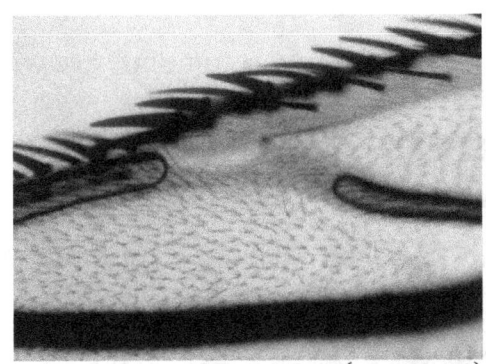
House-fly wing magnified 250x
Amanda Tear (CC BY-SA 4.0)

ered with hairs that excrete at the tips, a sticky fluid. Because of the hairs on its feet, the fly becomes a carrier of microbes and a menace to health.

The greatest grudge I have against this little, persistent companion of our household is the way it has misled us by appearing to be so fastidious in its personal habits. We have all of us seen, with curiosity and admiration, its complex ablutions and brushings. It usually begins, logically, with its front feet, the hands; these it cleans by rubbing them against each other lengthwise. The hairs and spines on one leg act as a brush for the other, and then lest they be not clean, it nibbles them with its rasping disc, which is all the teeth it has. It then cleans its head with these clean hands, rubbing them over its big eyes with a vigor that makes us wink simply to contemplate; then bobbing its head down so as to reach what is literally its back hair, it brushes valiantly. After this is done, it reaches forward first one and then the other foot of the middle pair of legs, and taking each in turn between the front feet, brushes it vigorously, and maybe nibbles it. But as a pair of military brushes, its hind feet are conspicuously efficient; they clean each other by being rubbed together and then they work simultaneously on each side in cleaning the wings, first the under side and then the upper side. Then over they come and comb the top of the thorax; then they brush the sides, top and under sides of the abdomen, cleaning each other between the acts.

Who, after witnessing all this, could believe that the fly could leave any tracks on our food, which would lead to our undoing! But the house-fly, like many housekeepers with the best intentions in the matter of keeping clean, has not mastered the art of getting rid of the microbes. Although it has so many little eyes, none of them can magnify a germ so as to make it visible; and thus it is that, when feeding around where there have been cases of typhoid and other enteric diseases, the house-fly's lit-

Empty pupa skin of fly, enlarged

These pupae were killed by parasitic wasp larvae

tle claws become infested with disease germs; and when it stops some day to clean up on our table, it leaves the germs with us. Thus our only safety lies in the final extermination of this little nuisance.

It is astonishing how few people know about the growth of flies. People of the highest intelligence in other matters, think that a small fly can grow into a large one. A fly, when it comes from the pupa stage, is as large as it will ever be, the young stages of flies being maggots. The house-fly's eggs are little, white, elongated bodies about as large as the point of a pin. These are laid preferably in horse manure. After a few hours, they hatch into slender, pointed, white maggots which feed upon the excrement. After five or six days, the larval skin thickens, turns brown, making the insect look like a small grain of wheat. This is the pupal stage, which lasts about five days, and then the skin bursts open and the full-grown fly appears. Of course, not all the flies multiply according to the example given to the children. The house-fly has many enemies and, therefore, probably no one hibernating mother fly is the ancestress of billions by September; however, despite enemies, flies multiply with great rapidity.

I know of no more convincing experiment as an example of the dangerous trail of the fly, than that of letting a house-fly walk over a saucer of nutrient gelatin. After three or four days, each track is plainly visible as a little white growth of bacteria.

Much is being done now to eradicate the house-fly, and undoubtedly there will be new methods of fighting it devised every year. The teacher should keep in touch with the bulletins on this subject published by the United States Department of Agriculture, and should give the pupils instructions according to the latest ideas. At present the following are the methods of fighting this pest: Keep the stable clean and place the manure under cover. All of the windows of the house should be well screened. All the flies which get into the house should be killed by using the commercial fly papers.

Lesson

Leading thought— The house-fly has conquered the world and is found everywhere. It breeds in filth and especially in horse manure. It is very prolific; the few flies that manage to pass the winter in this northern climate, are ancestors of the millions which attack us and our food later in the season. These are a menace to health because they carry germs of disease from sputa and excrementitious matter to our tables, leaving them upon our food.

Pavel Krok (cc by-sa 3.0)
Housefly larva

Method— Give out the questions for observation and let the pupils answer them either orally or in their note-books. If possible, every pupil should look at a house-fly through a three-quarters objective. If this is not possible, pictures should be shown to demonstrate its appearance.

Observations—

1. Look at a fly, using a lens if you have one. Describe its eyes. Do you see that they have a honeycomb arrangement of little eyes? Can you see, on top of the head between the big eyes, a dot? A microscope reveals this dot to be made of three tiny eyes, huddled together. After seeing a fly's eyes, do you wonder that you have so much difficulty in hitting it or catching it?

2. Can you see the fly's antennae? Do you think that it has a keen sense of smell? Why?

3. How many wings has the fly? How does it differ from the bee in this respect? Can you see two little white objects, one just behind the base of each wing? These are called poisers, or balancers, and all flies have them in some form. What is the color of the wings? Are they transparent? Can you see the veins in them? On what part of the body do the wings grow?

4. Look at the fly from below. How many legs has it? From what part of the body do the legs come? What is that part of the insect's body called, to which the legs and wings are attached?

5. How does the fly's abdomen look? What is its color and its covering?

6. Look at the fly's legs. How many segments can you see in a leg? Can you see that the segment on which the fly walks has several joints? Does it walk on all of these segments or on the one at the tip?

7. When the fly eats, can you see its tongue? Can you feel its tongue when it rasps your hand? Where does it keep its tongue usually?

8. Describe how a fly makes its toilet as follows: How does it clean its front feet? Its head? Its middle feet? Its hind feet? Its wings?

9. Do you know how flies carry disease? Did you ever see them making their toilet on your food at the table? Do you know what diseases are carried by flies? What must you do to prevent flies from bringing disease to your family?

10. Do you think that a small fly ever grows to be a large fly? How do the young of all kinds of flies look? Do you know where the house-fly lays its eggs? On what do the maggots feed? How long before they change to pupae? How long does it take them to grow from eggs to flies? How do the house-flies in our northern climate pass the winter?

11. *Lesson in Arithmetic*— It requires perhaps twenty days to span the time from the eggs of one generation of the house-fly to the eggs of the next, and thus there might easily be five generations in one summer. Supposing the fly which wintered behind the window curtain in your home last winter, flew out to the stables about May 1st and laid 120 eggs in the sweepings from the horse stable, all of which hatched and matured. Supposing one-half of these were mother flies and each of them, in turn, laid 120 eggs, and so on for five generations, all eggs laid developing into flies, and one-half of the flies of each generation being mother flies. How many flies would the fly that wintered behind your curtain have produced by September?

12. Pour some gelatin unsweetened, on a clean plate. Let a house-fly walk around on the gelatin as soon as it is cool; cover the plate to keep out the dust and leave it for two or three days. Examine it then and see if you can tell where the fly walked. What did it leave in its tracks?

13. Write an essay on the house-fly, its dangers and how to combat it, basing the essay on Bulletins of the U. S. Department of Agriculture.

The Colorado Potato-Beetle

TEACHER'S STORY

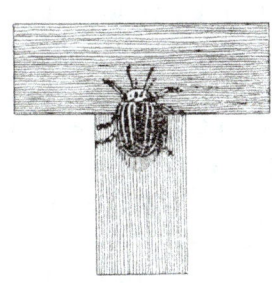

HE potato-beetle is not a very attractive insect, but it has many interesting peculiarities. No other common insect so clearly illustrates the advantage of warning colors. If we take a beetle in the hand, it at first promptly falls upon its back, folds its legs and antennae down close to its body, and "plays possum" in a very canny manner. But if we squeeze it a little, immediately an orange-red liquid is ejected on the hand, and a very ill-smelling liquid it is. If we press lightly, only a little of the secretion is thrown off; but if we squeeze harder it flows copiously. Thus a bird trying to swallow one of these beetles, would surely get a large dose. The liquid is very distasteful to birds, and it is indeed a stupid bird that does not soon learn to let severely alone orange and yellow beetles, striped with black. The source of this offensive and defensive juice is at first a mystery, but if we observe closely we can see it issuing along the hind edge of the thorax and the front portion of the wing-covers; the glands in these situations secrete the protective juice as it is needed. The larvae are also equipped with similar glands and, therefore, have the brazen habit of eating the

A lady beetle eating the eggs of a potato-beetle

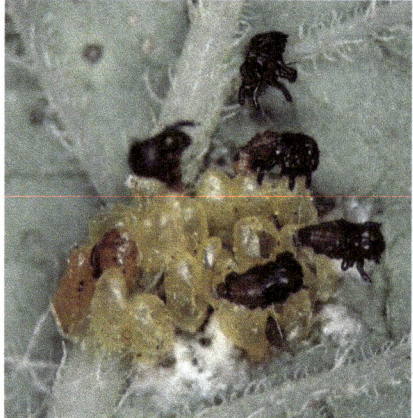
First stage larva of a potato-beetle

Pupa of a potato-beetle

leaves of our precious potatoes without attempting to hide. They seem to know that they are far safer when seen by birds than when concealed from them.

The life history of the potato-beetle is briefly as follows: Some of the adult beetles or pupae winter beneath the surface of the soil, burrowing down a foot or more to escape freezing. As soon as the potato plants appear above ground the mother beetle comes out and lays her eggs upon the under sides of the leaves. These orange-yellow eggs are usually laid in clusters. In about a week there hatches from the eggs little yellow or orange humpbacked larvae, which begin at once to feed upon the leaves. These larvae grow as do other insects, by shedding their skins. They do this four times, and during the last stages, are very conspicuous insects on the green leaves; they are orange or yellow with black dots along the sides, and so humpbacked are they that they seem to be "gathered with a puckering string" along the lower side. It requires from sixteen days to three weeks for a larva to complete its growth. It then descends into the earth and forms a little cell in which it changes to a pupa. It remains in this condition for one or two weeks, according to the temperature, and then the full-fledged beetle appears. The entire life cycle from egg to adult beetle may be passed in about a month, although if the weather is cold, this period will be longer. The beetles are very prolific, a mother beetle having been known to produce five hundred eggs, and there are two generations each year. These beetles not only damage the potato crop by stopping the growth through destroying the leaves, but they also cause the potatoes to be of inferior quality.

The adult beetle is an excellent object lesson in the study of beetle form. Attention should be called to the three regions of the body: A head which is bright orange; the compound eyes, which are black; and three simple eyes on the top of the head, which are difficult to see without a lens. The antennae are short, their joints easily noted, and special attention should be paid to their use, for they are constantly moving to feel approaching objects. The two pairs of mouth palpi may be seen, and the beetle will eagerly eat raw potatoes, so that the pupils may see that it has biting mouth-parts. The thoracic shield is orange, ornamented with black. The three pairs of legs are short, which is a proof that these beetles do not migrate on foot. The claws and the pads beneath can be seen with the naked eye. Each wing-cover bears five yellow stripes, also five black ones, although the outside black stripe is rather narrow. These beetles are very successful flyers. During flight, the wing-covers are raised and held motionless while the gauzy wings beneath are unfolded and do the work. Children are always interested in seeing the way the beetles fold their wings beneath the wing-covers.

One of the most remarkable things about the Colorado potato-beetle is its history. It is one of the few insect pests which is native to America. It formerly fed upon sandbur, a wild plant allied to the potato, which grows in the region of Colorado, Arizona and Mexico, and was a well behaved, harmless insect. With the advance of civilization westward, the potato came also, and proved to be an acceptable plant to this insect; and here we have an example of what an unlimited food supply will do for an insect species. The beetles multiplied so much faster than their parasites, that it seemed at one time as if they would conquer the earth by moving on from potato field to potato field. They started on their march to the Atlantic seaboard in 1859; in 1874, they reached the coast and judging by the numbers washed ashore, they sought to fly or swim across the Atlantic. By 1879, they had spread over an area consisting of more than

Biscan (CC BY-SA 3.0)
Children catching potato beetles to try and stop their spread

one-third of the United States.

Reference— The Colorado Potato-Beetle, Chittenden, Bulletin of U. S. Department of Agriculture.

Lesson

Leading thought— The Colorado potato-beetle is a very important insect, since it affects the price of potatoes each year. It is disagreeable as a food for birds, because of an acrid juice which it secretes. We should learn its life-history and thus be able to deal with it intelligently in preventing its ravages.

Method— The study of the potato-beetle naturally follows and belongs to gardening. The larvae should be brought into the schoolroom and placed in a breeding cage on leaves of the potato vine. Other plants may be put into the cage to prove that these insects will only eat the potato. The children should observe how the larvae eat and how many leaves a full grown larva will destroy in a day. Earth should be put in the bottom of the breeding cage so that the children may see the larvae descend and burrow into it. The adult beetles should be studied carefully, and especially, the children should see the excretion of the acrid juice.

Observations—

1. At what time do you see the potato-beetles? Why are they more numerous in the fall than in the spring? Where do those which we find in the spring come from? What will they do if they are allowed to live?

2. What is the shape of the potato-beetle? Describe the markings on its head. What color are its eyes? Describe its antennae. How are they constantly used? Can you see the palpi of the mouth? Give the beetle a bit of potato and note how it eats.

3. What is the color of the shield of the thorax? Describe the legs. Do you think the beetle can run fast? Why not? How many segments has the foot? Describe the claws. Describe how it clings to the sides of a tumbler or bottle.

Udo Schmidt (cc by-sa 2.0)

4. If the beetle cannot run rapidly, how does it travel? Describe the wing-covers. Why is this insect called the ten-lined potato beetle?

5. Describe the wings. How are they folded when at rest? How are the wing-covers carried when the beetle is flying?

6. Take a beetle in your hand. What does it do? Of what advantage is it to the insect to pretend that it is dead? If you squeeze the beetle what happens? How does the fluid which it ejects look and smell? Try and discover where this fluid comes from. Of what use is it to the beetle? Why will birds not eat the potato-beetle?

7. Where does the mother beetle lay her eggs? Are they laid singly or in clusters? What color are the eggs? How long after they are laid before they hatch?

8. Describe the young larva when it first hatches. What color is it at first? Does it change color later? Describe the colors and markings of a full grown larva.

9. How does this larva injure the potato vines? Does it remain in sight while it is feeding? Does it act as if it were afraid of birds? Why is it not eaten by birds?

10. Where does the larva go when it is full grown? How many times does it shed its skin during its growth? Does it make a little cell in the ground? How does the pupa look? Can you see in it the eyes, antennae, legs and wings of the beetle?

11. Write an English theme giving the history of the Colorado potato-beetle, and the reasons for its migration from its native place.

The Ladybird

Teacher's Story
Ladybird, Ladybird, fly away home!
Your house is on fire, your children are burning.

THIS incantation we, as children, repeated to this unhearing little beetle, probably because she is and ever has been, the incarnation of energetic indecision. She runs as fast as her short legs can carry her in one direction, as if her life depended on getting there, then she turns about and goes with quite as much vim in another direction. Thus, it is no wonder the children think that when she hears this news of her domestic disasters, she wheels about and starts for home; but she has not any home now nor did she ever have a home, and she does not carry even a trunk. Perhaps it would be truer to say that she has a home everywhere, whether she is cuddled under a leaf for a night's lodging or industriously climbing out on twigs, only to scramble back again, or perchance to take flight from their tips.

There are many species of ladybirds, but in general they all resemble a tiny pill cut in half, with legs attached to the flat side. Sometimes it may be a round and sometimes an oval pill, but it is always shining and the colors are always dull dark red, or yellow, or whitish, and black. Sometimes she is black with red or yellow spots, sometimes red or yellow with black spots and the spots are usually on either side of the thorax and one on each snug little wing-cover. But if we look at the ladybird carefully we can see the head and the short, clublike antennae. Behind the head is the thorax with its shield, broadening toward the rear, spotted and ornamented in various ways; the head and thorax together occupy scarcely a fourth of the length of the insect, and the remainder consists of the hemispherical body, encased with polished wing-covers. The little black legs, while quite efficient because they can be moved so rapidly, are not the ladybird's only means of locomotion; she is a good flier and has a long pair of dark wings which she folds cross-wise under her wing-covers. It is comical to see her pull up her wings, as a lady tucks up a long petticoat; and sometimes ladybird is rather slovenly about it and runs around with the tips of her wings hanging out behind, quite untidily.

©ENTOMART

The pupa and larva of a ladybird

Ladybird larva

But any untidiness must be inadvertent, because the ladybird takes very good care of herself and spends much time in "washing up." She begins with her front legs, cleaning them with her mandibles, industriously nibbling off every grain of dust; she then cleans her middle and hind legs by rubbing the two on the same side, back and forth against each other, each acting as a whisk broom for the other; she cleans her wings by brushing them between the edges of the wing-cover above and the tarsus of her hind leg below.

The ladybird is a clever little creature, even if it does

Ladybird pupa

Ladybird eggs with a match-head for scale
BÖHRINGER FRIEDRICH (CC BY-SA 2.5)

look like a pill, and if you disturb it, it will fold up its legs and drop as if dead, playing possum in a most deceptive manner. It will remain in this attitude of rigid death for at least a minute or two and then will begin to claw the air with all its six legs in an effort to turn right side up.

From our standpoint the ladybird is of great value, for during the larval as well as adult stages, all species except one, feed upon those insects which we are glad to be rid of. They are especially fond of aphids and scale insects. One of the greatest achievements of economic entomology was the introduction on the Pacific Coast of the ladybird from Australia, called the Vedalia, which preys upon the cottony cushion scale insect, a species very dangerous to orange and lemon trees. Within a few years the introduced ladybirds had completely exterminated this pest.

The ladybird's history is as follows: The mother beetle, in the spring, lays her eggs here and there on plants: as soon as the larva hatches, it starts out to hunt for aphids and other insects. It is safe to say that no ladybird would recognize her own children in time to save them, even if the house were burning, for they do not in the least resemble her; they are neither roly-poly nor shiny, but are long and segmented and velvety, with six queer, short legs that look and act as if they were whittled out of wood; they seem only efficient for clinging around a stem. The larvae are usually black, spotted with orange or yellow; there are six warts on each segment, which make the creature's back look quite rough. The absorbing business of the larva is to crawl around on plants and chew up the foolish aphids or the scale insects. I have seen one use its front foot to push an aphid, which it was eating, closer to its jaws; but when one green leg of its victim still clung to its head, it did not try to rub it off as its mother would have done, but twisted its head over this way and that, wiping off the fragment on a plant stem and then gobbling it up.

After the larva has shed its skeleton skin several times, and destroyed many times its own bulk of insects, it hunts for some quiet corner, hangs itself up by the tail and condenses itself into a sub-globular form; it sheds its spiny skin pushing it up around the point of attachment, and there lets it stay like the lion's skin of Hercules. As a pupa, it is more nearly rectangular than round, and if we look closely, we can see the wing-cases, the spotted segments of the abdomen, and the eyes, all encased in the pupa skin; the latter bursts open after a few days and the shining, little half-globe emerges a full-grown ladybird, ready for hiding in some cozy spot to pass the winter, from which she will emerge in the spring, to stock our trees and vines, next year, with her busy little progeny.

References— American Insects, Kellogg; Manual for the Study of Insects, Comstock.

CLINTON & CHARLES ROBERTSON (CC BY-SA 2.5)
Ladybird with wings spread about to take flight

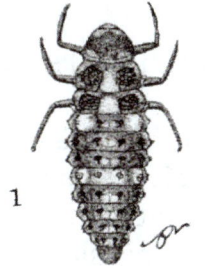

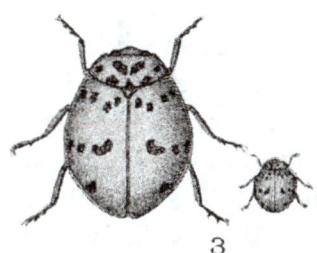

1, Larva; 2, pupa and 3, adult of a species of ladybird, enlarged. The small beetle represents actual size

LESSON

Leading thought— The ladybird is a beetle. Its young are very different from the adult in appearance, and feed upon plant-lice.

Method— These little beetles are very common in autumn and may be brought to the schoolroom and passed around in vials for the children to observe. Their larvae may be found on almost any plant infested with plant-lice. Plant and all may be brought into the schoolroom and the actions of the larvae noted by the pupils during recess.

Observations—

1. How large is the ladybird? What is its shape? Would two of them make a little globe if they were put flat sides together?

2. What colors do you find on your ladybird?

3. Do you see the ladybird's head and antennae? What is the broad shield directly back of the head called? How is it marked, and with what colors? What color are the wing-covers? Are there any spots upon them? How many? Does the ladybird use its wing-covers when it flies? Describe her true wings. Does she fold them beneath the wing-covers?

4. Note the legs and feet. Are the legs long? Are they fitted for running? To which part of the body are they attached?

5. If you disturb the ladybird how does she "play possum?" Describe how she makes her toilet.

THE LARVA

1. Describe the ladybird larva. Does it look like its mother? What is its form? Is it warty and velvety or shiny?

2. Describe its head and jaws as far as you can see. How does it act when eating? Can you see its little stiff legs? Is there a claw at the end of each?

3. Describe the actions of the ladybird larva in attacking and eating the plant-lice. Does it shed its skin as it grows?

4. Watch a larva until it changes to a pupa. How does the pupa look? Can you see the shed skin? Where is it? To what is the pupa attached? When the pupa skin breaks open what comes out of it?

5. Why is the ladybird of great use to us? Write an English theme upon the ladybird, called Vedalia, which saved the orange orchards of California.

Bruce Marlin (CC BY-SA 2.5)

The Firefly

TEACHER'S STORY
And lavishly to left and right,
The fireflies, like golden seeds,
Are sown upon the night.

—RILEY.

THE time of this sowing is during warm, damp nights in July and August, and even in September, although they are sown less lavishly then. How little most of us know of the harvest, although we see the sowing which begins in the early twilight against the background of tree shadows, and lasts until the cold atmosphere of the later night dampens the firefly ardor! There is a difference in species as to the height from the ground of their flight; some species hover next to the grass, others fly above our heads, but rarely as high as the tree tops in northern latitudes. Some species give a short flash that might be called a refulgent blinking; others give a longer flash so that we get an idea of the direction of their flight; and there is a common species in the Gulf States which gives such long flashes that they mark the night with gleaming curlicues.

It is likely to be an exciting chase, before we are able to capture a few of these insects for closer inspection; but when once captured, they do not sulk but will keep on with their flashing and give us a most edifying display. The portion of the firefly which gives the light is in the abdomen, and it glows steadily like "phosphorescent wood"; then suddenly it gleams with a green light that is strong enough to reveal all its surroundings; and it is so evidently an act of will on the part of the beetle, that it is startling to members of our race, who cannot even blush or turn pale voluntarily. The fireflies may be truly said to be socially brilliant, for the flashing of their lights is for the attraction of their mates.

EMMANUELM (CC BY-SA 3.0)
Two photos of a firefly, the first with a flash, the second with only its natural illumination

The fireflies are beetles, and there are many species which are luminous. A common one is here figured *(Photinus pyralis)*. It is pale gray above and the head is completely hidden by the big shield of the thorax. The legs are short; thus this beetle trusts mostly to its wings as a means of locomotion. The antennae are rather long and are kept in constant motion, evidently conveying intelligence of surroundings to the insect. Beneath the gray elytra, or wing-covers, is a pair of large, dark-veined membranous wings which are folded in a very neat manner crosswise and lengthwise, when not in use. When in use, the wing-covers are lifted stiffly and the flying is done wholly with the membranous wings. Looked at from beneath, we can at once see that some of the segments of the abdomen are partly or entirely sulphur yellow, and we recognize them as the lamp. If the specimen is a male, the yellow area covers all

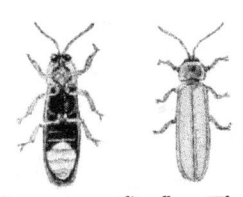

A common firefly—The view of the lower side shows the "lamp"

Larva and pupa of a common firefly

of the end of the abdomen up to the fourth or fifth segment; but if it is a female, only the middle portion of the abdomen, especially the fifth segment, is converted into a lamp. These yellow areas, when dissected under the microscope, prove to be filled with fine tracheae or air-tubes; and although we know very little about the way the light is made, it is believed that by flooding the tubes with air, the oxygen in some way produces the light.

In some species, the female is wingless and has very short wing-covers, and a portion of her body emits a steady, greenish light which tells her lord and master where to find her. These wingless females are called glow-worms.

Fireflies during their larval stages are popularly called wire worms, although there are many other beetle larvae thus called. In many of the species, the firefly eggs, larvae and pupae are all luminescent, but not so brilliant as when adults. The larva of the species here figured, was studied by C. V. Riley, who gave us an interesting account of its habits. It lives in the ground and feeds on soft-bodied insects, probably earth-worms. Each segment of this wire worm has a horny, brown plate above, with a straight white line running through the middle and a slightly curved white line on each side; the sides of the larva are soft and rose-colored; the white spiracles show against little, oval, brown patches. Beneath, the larva is cream color with two brown comma-like dots at the center of each segment. The head can be pulled back completely beneath the first segment. The most interesting thing about this larva is the prop-leg at the end of its body, which naturally aids it in locomotion; but this prop-leg also functions as a brush; after the larva has become soiled with too eager delving into the tissues of some earthworm, it curls its body over, and with this fan-shaped hind foot scrubs its head and face very clean. This is a rare instance of a larva paying any attention to its toilet.

When full-grown, the larva makes a little oval cell within the earth and changes to a pupa; after about ten days, the pupa skin is shed and

Giuseppe ME (CC BY-SA 3.0)
Female firefly larva showing the light emitting organs on its abdomen

the full-fledged beetle comes forth. The larva and pupa of this species give off light, but are not so brilliant as the adult. The pupils should be encouraged to study the early stages of the fireflies, because very little is known concerning them.

In Cuba a large beetle called the cucujo has two great oval spots on its thorax, resembling eyes, which give off light. The Cuban ladies wear cucujos at the opera, in nets, in the hair. I once had a pair which I tethered with gold chains to the bodice of my ball gown. The eye-spots glowed steadily, but with the movement of dancing, they grew more brilliant until no glittering diamonds could compete with their glow.

Lesson

Leading thought— When the firefly wishes to make a light, it can produce one that, if we knew how to make, would greatly reduce the price of artificial light; for the light made by fireflies and other creatures, requires less energy than any other light known.

Method— After the outdoor observations have been made, collect some of these beetles in the evening with a sweep net; place them under a glass jar or tumbler, so that their light can be studied at close range. The next day give the observation lesson on the insects.

Observations—

1. At what time of year do you see fireflies? Do they begin to lighten before it is dark? Do you see them high in the air or near the ground? Is the flash they give short, or long enough to make a streak of light? Do you see them on cold and windy nights or on warm, still, damp evenings? Make a note of the hour when you see the first one flash in an evening.

JUD MCCRANIE (CC BY-SA 4.0)
An eight second exposure of fireflies in Goergia

2. Catch a few fireflies in the night; put them under a glass jar. Can you see the light when they are not flashing? What color is it? When they make the flash can you see the outline of the "firefly lamp?" Watch closely and see if you think the flashing is a matter of will on the part of the firefly. Do you think the firefly is signaling to his mate when he flashes?

3. Study the firefly in daylight. Is it a fly or is it a beetle? What color is it above? When you look squarely down upon it, can you see its head and eyes?

4. Are the firefly's legs long or short? When a beetle has short legs is it a sign that it usually walks, runs or flies?

5. Describe the antennae. Are they in constant motion? What service do you think the firefly's antennae perform for it?

6. Lift one of the wing-covers carefully. What do you find beneath it? Does the beetle use its wing-covers to beat the air and help it during flight? How does the beetle hold its wing-covers when flying?

7. Turn the beetle on its back. Can you see the part of the body that flashes? What color is it?

8. Do you know the life history of the firefly? What is it like in its earlier stages? Where does it live? Does it have the power of making light when it is in the larval stage?

> "There, in warm August gloaming,
> With quick silent brightenings,
> From meadow-lands roaming,
> The firefly twinkles
> His fitful heat-lightnings."
>
> —LOWELL.

The Ways of the Ant

My child, behold the cheerful ant,
How hard she works, each day;
She works as hard as adamant
Which is very hard, they say.

—OLIVER HERFORD.

VERY many performances on the part of the ant seem to us without reason; undoubtedly many of our performances seem likewise to her. But the more understandingly we study her and her ways, the more we are forced to the conclusion that she knows what she is about; I am sure that none of us can sit down by an ant-nest and watch its citizens come and go, without discovering things to make us marvel.

By far the greater number of species of ants find exit from their underground burrows, beneath stones in fields. They like the stone for more reasons than one; it becomes hot under the noon sun and remains warm during the night, thus giving them a cozy nursery in the evening for their young. Some species make mounds, and often several neighboring mounds belong to the same colony, and are connected by underground galleries. There are usually several openings into these mounds. In case of some of the western species which make galleries beneath the ground, there is but one opening to the nest and Dr. McCook says that this gate is closed at night; at every gate in any ants' nest, there are likely to be sentinels stationed, to give warning of intruders.

As soon as a nest is disturbed, the scared little citizens run helter skelter to get out of the way; but if there are any larvae or pupae about, they are never too frightened to take them up and make off with them; but when too hard pressed, they will in most cases drop the precious burden, although I have several times seen an ant, when she dropped a pupa, stand guard over it and refuse to budge without it. The ant's eggs are very small objects, being oblong and about the size of a pin point. The larvae are translucent creatures, like rice grains with one end pointed. The pupae are yellowish, covered with a parchment-like sac, and resemble grains of wheat. When we lift stones in a field, we usually find directly beneath, the young of a certain size.

BROCKEN INAGLORY (CC BY-SA 3.0)
Ants trapped in amber

There are often, in the same species of ants, two sizes; the large ones are called majors and the smaller minors; sometimes there is a smaller size yet, called minims. The smaller sizes are probably the result of lack of nutrition. But whatever their size, they all work together to bring food for the young and in caring for the nest. We often see an ant carrying a dead insect or some other object larger than herself. If she cannot lift it or shove it, she turns around, and going backwards, pulls it along. It is rarely that we see two carrying the same load, although we have observed this several times. In one or two cases, the two seemed not to be in perfect accord as to which path to take. If the ants find some large supply of food, many of them will form a procession to bring it into the nest bit by bit; such processions go back by making a little detour so as not to meet and interfere with those coming. During most of the year, an ant colony consists only of workers and laying queens, but in early summer the nest may be found swarming with winged forms which are the kings and queens. Some warm day these will issue from the nest

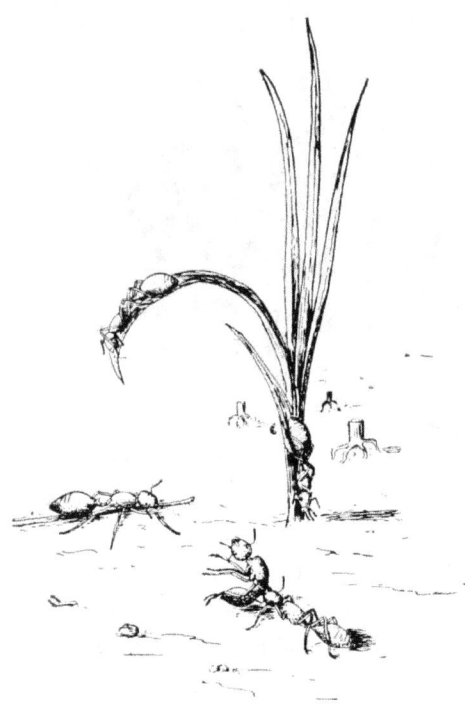

Agricultural ants. Note that one ant is carrying a sister

and take their marriage flight, the only time in their lives when they use their wings; for ants, like seeds, seem to be provided with wings simply for the sake of scattering wide the species. It is a strange fact, that often on the same day swarms will issue from all the nests of one species in the whole region; by what mysterious messenger, word is sent that brings about this unanimous exodus, is still a mystery to us. This seems to be a provision for cross-breeding; and as bearing upon this, Miss Fielde discovered that an alien king is not only made welcome in a nest, but is sometimes seized by workers and pulled into a nest; this is most significant, since no worker of any other colony of the same species, is permitted to live in any but its own nest.

After the marriage flight, the ants fall to the ground and undoubtedly a large number perish; however, just here our knowledge is lamentably lacking, and observations on the part of pupils as to what happens to these winged forms will be valuable. In the case of most species, we know that a queen finds refuge in some shelter and there lays eggs. Mr. Comstock once studied a queen of the big, black carpenter ant which lives under the bark of trees. This queen, without taking any food herself, was able to lay her eggs and rear her first brood to maturity; she regurgitated food for this first brood, and then they went out foraging for the colony. However, Miss Fielde found that in the species she studied, the queen could not do this; a question most interesting to solve is whether any of the young queens, after the marriage flight, are adopted into other colonies of the same species. As soon as a queen begins laying eggs, she sheds her then useless wings, laying them aside as a bride does her veil.

Jens Buurgaard Nielsen (cc by-sa 3.0)
Black garden ant queen with, and without wings

When we are looking for ants' nests beneath stones, we often stumble upon a colony consisting of citizens differing in color. One has the head and thorax rust-red with the abdomen and legs brown; associated with this brown ant, is a black or ash-colored species. These black ants are the slaves of the brown species; but slavery in the ant world has its ameliorations. When the slave makers attack the slave nest, they do not fight the inmates unless they are obliged to. They simply loot the nest of the larvae or pupae, which they carry off to their own nests; and there they are fed and reared, as carefully as are their own young. The slaves seem to be perfectly contented, and conduct the household affairs of their masters with apparent cheerfulness. They do all the taking care of the nest and feeding the young, but they are never permitted to go out with war parties; thus they never fight, unless their colony is attacked by marauders.

If one chances upon an ant battle, one must needs compare it to a battle of men before the invention of gunpowder; for in those days fighting was more gory and dreadful than now, since man fought man until one of the twain was slain. There is a great variation in military skill as well as in courage shown by different species of ants; the species most skilled in warfare, march to battle in a solid column and when they meet the enemy, the battle resolves itself into duels, although there is no code of ant honor which declares that one must fight the enemy single-handed. Although some ants are provided with venomous stings, our common species use their jaws for weapons; they also eject upon each other a very acid liquid which we know as formic acid. Two enemies approach each other, rear on their hind legs, throw this ant vitriol at each other, then close in deadly combat, each trying to cut the other in two. Woe to

FIR0002 (GFDL 1.2)

Meat eater ant nest during swarming

the one on which the jaws of her enemy are once set! For the ant has bull-dog qualities, and if she once gets hold, she never lets go even though she be rent in pieces herself. At night the ant armies retreat to their citadels, but in the morning fare forth again to battle; and thus the war may be waged for days, and the battlefield be strewn with the remains of the dead and dying. So far as we are able to observe, there are two chief causes for ant wars; one is when two colonies desire the same ground, and the other is for the purpose of making slaves.

Perhaps the most interesting as well as most easily observed of all ant practices, are those that have to do with plant-lice, or aphids. If we find an ant climbing a plant of any sort, it is very likely that we shall find she is doing it for the purpose of tending her aphid herds. The aphid is a stupid little creature which lives by thrusting its bill or sucking tube into a stem or leaf of a plant, and thus settles down for life, nourished by the sap which it sucks up; it has a peculiar habit of exuding from its alimentary canal drops of honey-dew, when it feels the caress of the ant's antennae upon its back. I had one year under observation, a nest of elegant little ants with shining triangular abdomens which they waved in the air like pennants when excited. These ants were most devoted attendants on the plant-lice infesting an evening primrose; if I jarred the primrose stem, the ants had a panic, and often one would seize an aphid in her jaws and dash about madly, as if to rescue it at all hazards. When the ant wishes honey-dew, she approaches the aphid, stroking it or patting it gently with her antennae, and if a drop of the sweet fluid is not at once forthcoming, it is probably because other ants have previously exhausted its individual supply; if the ant gets no response, she hurries on to some other aphid not yet milked dry.

Viamoi (CC BY-SA 2.0)
An ant tending to its aphids

This devotion of ants to aphids has been known for a hundred years, but only recently has it been discovered to be of economic importance. Professor Forbes, in studying the corn root-louse, discovered that the ants care for the eggs of this aphid in their own nests during the winter, and take the young aphids out early in the spring, placing them on the roots of smartweed; later, after the corn is planted, the ants move their charges to the roots of the corn. Ants have been seen to give battle to the enemies of the aphid. The aphids of one species living on dogwood are protected while feeding by stables, which a certain species of ant builds around them, from a mortar made of earth and vegetable matter.

References— *Ants*, W. M. Wheeler; *Ant Communities*, McCook.

Lesson

Leading thought— However aimless to us may seem the course of the ant as we see her running about, undoubtedly if we understood her well enough, we should find that there is rational ant-sense in her performances. Therefore, whenever we are walking and have time, let us make careful observations as to the actions of the ants which we may see.

Method— The following questions should be written on the

IronChris (CC BY-SA 3.0)
Carrying a spider's mandible

Black garden ant nest
MARCUS33 (CC BY-SA 3.0)

blackboard and copied by the pupils in their note-books. This should be done in May or June, and the answers to the questions worked out by observations made during the summer vacation.

Observations—

1. Where do you find ants' nests? Describe all the different kinds you have found. In what sort of soil do they make their nests? Describe the entrance to the nest. If the nest is a mound, is there more than one entrance? Are there many mounds near each other? If so, do you think they all belong to the same colony?

2. When the nest is disturbed, how do the ants act? Do they usually try to save themselves alone? Do they seek to save their young at the risk of their own lives? If an ant, carrying a young one is hard pressed, will she drop it?

3. Make notes on the difference in appearance of eggs, larvae and pupae in any ants' nest.

4. In nests under stones, can you find larvae and pupae assorted according to sizes?

5. How many sizes of ants do you find living in the same nest?

6. What objects do you find ants carrying to their nests? Are these for food? How does an ant manage to carry an object larger than herself? Do you ever see two ants working together carrying the same load?

7. If you find a procession of ants carrying food to their nest, note if they follow the same path coming and going.

8. If you find winged ants in a nest, catch a few in a vial with a few

of the workers, and compare the two. The winged ants are kings and queens, the kings being much smaller than the queens.

9. If you chance to encounter a swarm of winged ants taking flight, make observations as to the size of swarm, the height above the ground, and whether any are falling to the earth.

10. Look under the loose bark of trees for nests of the big, black carpenter ant. You may find in such situations a queen ant starting a colony, which will prove most desirable for stocking an artificial ant's nest.

11. If you find ants climbing shrubs, trees or other plants, look upon the leaves for aphids and note the following points:

a. How does an ant act as she approaches an aphid?

b. If the aphids are crowded on the leaf, does she step on them?

c. Watch carefully to see how the ant touches the aphid when she wishes the honey-dew.

d. Watch how the aphid excretes the honey-dew, and note if the ant eats it.

e. If you disturb aphids which have ants tending them, note whether the ants attempt to defend or rescue their herds.

f. If there are aphis-lions or ladybird larvae eating the aphids, note if the ants attack them.

12. If you find a colony of ants under stones where there are brown and black ants living together, the black members are the slaves of the brown. Observe as carefully as possible the actions of both the black and the brown inhabitants of the nest.

13. If you chance to see ants fighting, note how they make the attack. With what weapons do they fight? How do they try to get at the adversary?

14. Write an English theme covering the following points: How ants take their slaves; the attitude of masters and slaves toward each other; the work which the slaves do, and the story of the ant battle. How ants care for and use their herds.

References— *American Insects*, Kellogg, *Manual for the Study of Insects*, Comstock; *Ants*, McCook; *True Tales*, Jordan, page 6.

How To Make the Lubbock Ant-Nest

LESSON

Material— Two pieces of window glass, 10 inches square; a sheet of tin, 11 inches square; a piece of plank, 1¼ inch thick, 20 inches long and at least 16 inches wide; a sheet of tin or a thin, flat board, 10 inches square.

To make the nest— Take the plank and on the upper side, a short distance from the edge, cut a deep furrow. This furrow is to be filled with water, as a moat, to keep the ants imprisoned. It is necessary, therefore, that the plank should have no knot holes, and that it be painted thoroughly to keep it from checking. Take the sheet of tin 11 inches square, and make it into a tray by turning up the edges three-eighths of an inch. Place this tray in the middle of the plank. Place within the tray one pane of glass. Lay around the edges of this glass four strips of wood about half an inch wide and a little thicker than the height of the ants which are to live in the nest. Cover the glass with a thin layer of fine earth. Take the remaining pane of glass and cut a triangular piece off of one corner, then place the pane on top of the other, resting upon the pieces of wood around the sides. The cover of the nest may be a piece of tin, with a handle soldered to the center, or a board with a screw-eye in the center with which to lift it. There should be a piece of blotter or of very thin sponge, introduced into the nest between the two panes of glass, in a position where it may be reached with a pipette, without removing the upper glass, for it must be kept always damp.

To establish a colony in this nest proceed as follows: Take a two-quart glass fruit jar and a garden trowel. Armed with these, visit some pasture or meadow near by, and find under some stone, a small colony of ants which have plenty of eggs and larvae. Scoop up carefully eggs, ants, dirt and all and place in the jar, being as careful as possible not to injure the specimens. While digging, search carefully for the queen, which is a larger ant and is sometimes thus found. But if you have plenty of eggs, larvae and pupae, the ants will become very contented in their new nest while taking care of them. After you have taken all the ants desirable, place the cover on the jar, carry them to the Lubbock nest and carefully empty the contents of the fruit jar on top of the board which covers the nest. Of course the furrow around the plank has been filled with water, so the stragglers cannot escape. The ants will soon find the way into the nest through the cut corner of the upper pane of glass, and will transfer their larvae to it because it is dark. After they are in the nest, which should be within two or three hours, remove the dirt on the cover, and the nest is ready for observation. But, since light disturbs the little prisoners, the cover should be removed only for short periods.

The Fielde nest is better adapted for a serious study of ants, but it is not so well adapted for the schoolroom as is the Lubbock nest.

Reference—Ants, W. M. Wheeler.

A Lubbock ant-nest

An ant mound hold can prevent water entering the nest during rain

The Ant-Nest, and What May Be Seen within It

TEACHER'S STORY

NT anatomy becomes a very interesting study when we note the vigorous way the ant uses it—even to the least part. The slender waist characterizes the ant as well as the wasp; the three regions of the body are easily seen, the head with its ever moving antennae, the slender thorax with its three pairs of most efficient legs, and the long abdomen. The ant's legs are fairly long as compared with the size of the body and the ant can run with a rapidity that, comparatively, would soon outdistance any Marathon runner, however famed. I timed an ant one day when she was taking a constitutional on my foot rule. She was in no hurry, and yet she made time that if translated into human terms would mean 16 yards per second. In addition to running, many ants when frightened will make leaps with incredible swiftness.

The ant does not show her cleverness in her physiognomy, probably because her eyes seem small and dull and she has a decidedly "re-

A common ant

Fir0002/Flagstaffotos (GFDL v1.2)
The mandible of a bullant

treating forehead;" but the brain behind this unpromising appearance is far more active and efficient than that behind the gorgeous great eyes of the dragon-fly or behind the "high brow" of the grasshopper. The ant's jaws are very large compared with her head; they work sidewise like a pair of shears and are armed with triangular teeth along the biting edges; these are not teeth in a vertebrate sense, but are like the teeth of a saw. These jaws are the ant's chief utensils and weapons; with them she seizes the burdens of food which she carries home; with them she gently lifts her infant charges; with them she crushes and breaks up hard food; with them she carries out soil from her tunnel, and with them she fights her enemies. She also has a pair of long palpi, or feelers.

Although her eyes are so small and furnished with coarse facets, as compared with other insects, this fact need not count against her, for she has little need of eyes. Her home life is passed in dark burrows where her antennae give her information of her surroundings. Note how these antennae are always moving, seeming to be atremble in eagerness to receive sensations. But aside from their powers of telling things by the touch, wherein they are more delicate than the fingers of the blind, they have other sense organs which are comparable to our sense of smell. Miss Fielde has shown that the five end segments of the antennae have each its own powers in detecting odor. The end segment detects the odor of the ant's own nest and enables her to distinguish this from other nests. The next, or eleventh segment, detects the odor of any descendant of the same queen; by this, she recognizes her sisters wherever she finds them. Through the next, or tenth segment, she recognizes the odor of her own feet on the trail, and thus

Two worker ants communicating through touch and pheremones

can retrace her own steps. The eighth and ninth segments convey to her the intelligence and means of caring for the young. If an ant is deprived of these five end-joints of the antennae, she loses all power as a social ant and becomes completely disenfranchised. Miss Fielde gives her most interesting experiments in detail in the Proceedings of the Academy of Natural Sciences of Philadelphia, July and October, 1901.

It is natural enough that the ant, depending so much on her antennae for impressions and stimuli, should be very particular to keep them clean and in good order. She is well equipped to do this, for she has a most efficient antennae brush on her wrist; it is practically a circular comb, which just fits over the antenna; and to see the ants using these brushes is one of the most common sights in the ant-nest and one of the most amusing. The ant usually commences by lifting her leg over one antenna and deftly passing it through the brush, and then licks the brush clean by passing it through her mouth, as a cat washes her face; then she cleans the other in a similar manner and possibly finishes by doing both alternately, winding up with a flourish, like a European gentleman curling his mustaches. Her antennae

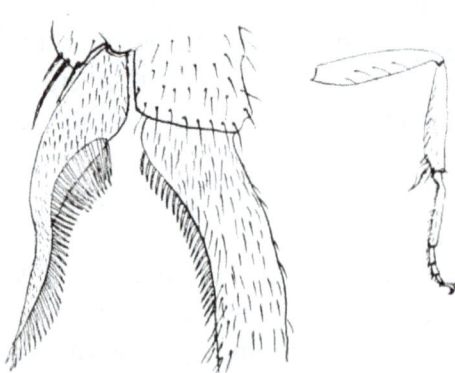
The antenna-comb on the front leg of an ant

cleaned, she starts promptly to do something, for she is a little six-footed Martha, always weighed down or buoyed up by many duties and cares. Keeping her antennae on the qui vive, she assures herself, by touch, of the nature of any obstacle in her path. If she meets another ant, their antennae cross and pat each other, and thus they learn whether they are sisters or aliens; if they are sisters, they may stand for some time with their antennae fluttering. One who has watched ants carefully, is compelled to believe that they thus convey intelligence of some sort, one to the other. The ant is a good sister "according to her lights;" if her sister is hungry, she will give to her, even from her own partially digested food; the two will often stand mouth to mouth for some minutes during this process; if she feels inclined, she will also help a sister at her toilet, and lick her with her tongue as one cow licks another. The tongue of the ant is very useful in several ways; with it she takes up liquids, and also uses it with much vigor as a washcloth. Sometimes an ant will spend a half hour or more at her own toilet, licking every part of her own body that her tongue can reach, meanwhile going through all sorts of contortions to accomplish it; she uses her feet to scrub portions of her body, not to be reached by her tongue.

Ants making their toilets

But it is as infant nurse that the ant is a shining example. No mother instinct is hers, for she has yielded the power of motherhood to the exigencies of business life, since all workers are females but are undeveloped sexually. She shows far more sense in the care of her infant sisters, than the mother instinct often supplies to human mothers. The ant nurse takes the eggs as soon as laid, and whether or not her care retards or hastens hatching we know not; but we do know, that although the queen ant may not lay more than two eggs per day, a goodly number of these seem to hatch at the same time. The eggs are massed in bundles and are sticky on the outside so as to hold the bundle together. Miss Fielde says, as the eggs are hatching, one ant will hold up the bundle, while another feeds those which have broken the shell. The larvae, when young, also hang together by means of tiny hooks on their bodies. This habit of the eggs and young larvae is a convenient one, since an ant is thus able to carry many at a time.

The larvae are odd looking little creatures, shaped like crookneck squashes, the small end being the head and neck and the latter being very extensible. The ant nurses, by feeding some more than others, are able to keep a brood at the same stage of development; and in a well ordered ant-nest, we find those of the same size in one nursery. I have often thought of a graded school as I have noted in ant-nests the youngsters assorted according to size.

The ants seem to realize the cost and care of rearing their young; and when a nest is attacked, the oldest, which are usually in the pupa stage, are saved first. When the larvae are young, they are fed on regurgitated food; but as they grow older, the food is brought to them, or they to the food, and they do their own eating. In one of my nests, I placed part of the yolk of an egg hard boiled, and the ant nurses dumped the larvae down around the edges of it; there they munched industriously, until through their transparent bodies I could see the yellow of the egg the whole length of the alimentary canal. The ant nurses are very particular about temperatures for their young, and Miss Fielde says they are even more careful about draughts. Thus they are obliged to move them about in the ground nests, carrying them down to the lower nurseries in the heat of the day, and bringing them up, nearer to the warm stones, during the evenings. This moving is always done carefully, and though the ant's jaws are such formidable nippers, she carries her baby sisters with gentleness; and if they be pupae, she holds them by the loose pupal skin, like carrying a baby by its clothes. The pupae look like plump little grain bags, tied at one end with a black string. They are the size of small grains of wheat, and are often called ants' eggs, which is absurd, since they are almost as large as the ant. Ants' eggs are not larger than pin points.

The ant nurses keep the larvae and pupae very clean by licking them; and when a youngster issues from the pupa skin, it is a matter of much interest to the nurses. I have often seen two or three of them help straighten out the cramped legs and antennae of the young one, and hasten to feed her with regurgitated food. When ants first issue

CHRISTIAN R. LINDER (CC BY-SA 3.0)
Queen leafcutter ant with larvae and workers

from the pupa skin they are pale in color, their eyes being very black in contrast; they are usually helpless and stupid, although they often try to clean their antennae and make a toilet; but they do not know enough to follow their elders from one room to another, and they are a source of much care to the nurses. In case of moving, a nurse will lock jaws with a "callow," as a freshly hatched adult ant is called, and drag her along, the legs of the callow sprawling helplessly meanwhile. If in haste, the nurse takes hold anywhere, by the neck or the leg, and hustles her charge along; if she takes her by the waist the callow curls up like a kitten, and is thus more easily moved. After moving them from one chamber to the next, I have noticed that the callows are herded together, their attendants ranged in a circle about them. Often we see one ant carrying another which is not a callow, and this means that a certain number of the colony have made up their minds to move, while the others are not awake to this necessity. In such a case, one of these energetic sisters will seize another by the waist, and carry her off with an air that says plainly, "Come along, you stupid!"

Ants are very cleanly in their nests, and we find the refuse piled in a heap at one corner, or as far as possible from the brood.

If we are fortunate enough to find a queen for the nest, then we

may observe the attention she gets; she is always kept in a special compartment, and is surrounded by ladies in waiting, who feed her and lick her clean and show solicitude for her welfare; although I have never observed in an ants' nest, that devotion to royalty which we see in a beehive.

Not the least interesting scene in an ants' nest is when all, or some, are asleep and are as motionless as if dead.

Lesson

Leading thought— The ants are very devoted to their young and perhaps the care of them is the most interesting feature in the study of the artificial nest.

Method— Have, in the schoolroom, a Lubbock's nest with a colony of ants within it, with their larvae in all stages, and if possible, their queen. For observing the form of the ant, pass one or two around in a vial.

Observations—

1. What is there peculiar about the shape of the ant's body? Can you see which section bears the legs? Are the ants' legs long compared

with her body? Can she run rapidly?

2. Look at the ant's head through a lens, and describe the antennae, the jaws and the eyes.

3. Note how the ant keeps her antennae in motion.

DAWIDI (CC BY 2.5)

An ant collects honeydew from an aphid

Note how she gropes with them as a blind person with his hands. Note how she uses them in conversing with her companions.

4. How does the ant clean her antennae? Does she clean them more often than any other part of her body? How does she make her toilet?

5. See how an ant eats syrup. How do ants feed each other?

6. How does the ant carry an object? How does she carry a larva or a pupa? Have you ever seen one ant carry another? If so, describe it.

7. Note the way the ants feed their young. How do they keep them clean? Does an ant carry one egg or one small larva at a time or a bundle of them? How do you suppose the bundle is fastened together?

8. Describe an egg, a larva and a pupa of the ant and tell how they differ. Do you know which ant is the mother of the larvae in the nest?

9. Do you find larvae of different sizes all together in your nest? Do you find larvae and pupae in the same group? Do the ants move the young often from one nest to another? Why do you suppose they do this?

10. Note how the ant nurses take care of the callow ant when it is coming out from the pupa skin. How do they assist her and care for her? How do they lead her around? How do ants look when resting?

11. Note where the ants throw the refuse from the nest. Do they ever change the position of this dump heap?

The Mud-Dauber

TEACHER'S STORY

THIS little cement worker is a nervous and fidgety creature, jerking her wings constantly as she walks around in the sunshine; but perhaps this is not nervousness, but rather to show off the rainbow iridescence of her black wings; surely such a slim-waisted being as she, has a right to be vain. No tight lacing ever brought about such a long, slim waist as hers; it is a mere pedicel and the abdomen is a mere knob at the end of it. The latter seen from the outside, would seem of little use as an abdomen; but if we watch the insect flying, we can see plainly that it is used to steer with.

In early summer, we find this black wasp at her trade as a mason. She seeks the edges of pools or puddles where she works industriously, leaving many little holes whence she takes mud to mix with the saliva, which she secretes from her mouth to make firm her cement. This cement she plasters on the under side of some roof or rafter or other protected place, going back and forth until she has built a suitable foundation. She works methodically, making a tube about an inch long, smooth inside but rough outside, the walls about one-eighth of an inch thick. She does all of the plastering with her jaws, which she uses as a trowel. When the tube is completed except that the end is left open, she starts off in quest of spiders, and very earnestly does she seek them. I have seen her hunt every nook and corner of a piazza for this prey. When she finds a spider, she pounces upon it and stings it until it is helpless, and carries it to her cement tube, which is indeed a spider sarcophagus, and thrusts it within. She brings more spiders until her tube is nearly full; she then lays an egg within it and then makes more cement and neatly closes the door of the tube. She then places another tube by the side of this, which she provisions and closes in the same way; and then she may make another and another tube, often a half dozen, under one adobe roof.

A mud-dauber and her nests, with cells cut open showing a, larva full frown; b, cocoon; c, young larva feeding on its spider-meat and d, and empty cell

The wasp in some mysterious way knows how to thrust her sting into the spider's nervous system in a peculiar way, which renders her victim unable to move although it yet lives. The wasp is no vegetarian like the bee, and she must supply her young with wasp-meat instead of bee-bread. Since it is during the summer and hot weather when the young wasps are hatched and begin their growth, their meat must be kept fresh for a period of two or three weeks. So these paralyzed spiders do not die, although they are helpless. It is certainly a practical joke with justice in it, that these ferocious creatures lie helpless while being eaten by a fat little grub which they would gladly devour, if they could move.

The wasp larva is a whitish, plump grub and it eats industriously until the spider meat is exhausted. It then weaves a cocoon of silk about itself which just covers the walls of its home tube, like a silken tapestry; within this cocoon the grub changes to a pupa. When it finally emerges, it is a full-grown wasp with jaws which are able to cut a door in the end of its tube, through which it comes out into the world, a free

Mud dauber wasp nest — Sukeerti Dwivedi (CC BY-SA 4.0)

and accepted mason. The females or queens, which issue late in the season, hide in warm or protected places during the winter; they particularly like the folds of lace window curtains for hibernating quarters. There they remain until spring comes, when they go off to build their plaster houses.

There are about seventy species of mud wasps in our country. Some provision their nests with caterpillars instead of spiders. This is true of the jug-builder, which makes her nest jug-shaped and places two or three of them side by side upon a twig. She uses hair in her mortar, which makes it stronger. This is necessary, since the jug is saddled upon twigs and is more exposed to the rain than is the nest of the most common mud-dauber. The jug-builder is brown in color and has yellow markings on the abdomen; but she does not resemble the yellowjackets, because she has a threadlike waist. There are other species of mud wasps which use any small cavity they can find for the nest, plastering up the opening after the nest has been provisioned and the egg laid. We often find keyholes, knot-holes and even the cavity in the telephone receiver, plastered up by these small opportunists.

The Jug-builder and her nests

The mud-dauber which is the most common, and most likely to be selected for this lesson, is a slender creature and looks as if she were made of black tinsel; her body gives off glints of steel and blue; her abdomen constantly vibrates with the movement of breathing. Her eyes are large and like black beads; her black antennae curve gracefully outward, and her wings, corrugated with veins, shimmer with a smoky blue, green and purple. She stands on her black tip-toes when she walks, and she has a way of turning around constantly as if she expected an attack from the rear. Her wings, like those of other mud-wasps, are not folded fan-wise like those of the yellow-jacket, but are folded by each other over her back.

Lesson

Leading thought— There are certain wasps which gather mud and mix it into mortar with which to build nests for their young. Within these nests, the mother wasp places spiders or insects which are disabled by her sting, for the food of the young wasps.

Method— Have the pupils bring the homes of the mud wasps to school for observation. The wasps themselves are very common in June and also in September, and they also may be studied at school and may be passed around in vials for closer observation; they do not sting severely when handled, the sting being a mere prick. The purpose of the lesson should be to stimulate the pupils to watch the mud-daubers while building their nests and capturing their prey.

Observations—

1. Where did you find the mud-dauber's nest? How was it protected from the rain? Was it easily removed? Could you remove it all, or did some of it remain stuck fast?

2. What is the shape of the nest? How does it look inside? Of how many tubes does it consist? How long is each tube? Were the tubes laid side by side?

3. Of what material was the nest made? Is it not much harder than mud? How did the wasp change the mud to cement? Where did she get the mud? How did she carry it? With what tools did she plaster it?

4. For what purpose was the nest made? Is the inside of the tubes smooth as compared with the outside of the nest?

5. Write a little story about all that happens in one of these tubes,

including the following points: What did the mother wasp place in the tube? How and why did she close it? What hatched from the egg she placed within it? How does the young wasp look? On what does it feed? What sort of a cocoon does it spin? How does it get out of the nest when full-grown?

6. Describe the mud-dauber wasp. How large is she? What is the color of her body? Of her wings? How many wings has she? How are her wings folded differently from those of the yellow-jacket? Describe her eyes; her antennae; her legs; her waist; her abdomen.

Pollinator (CC BY-SA 3.0)
An organ pipe mud dauber nest, showing different muds gathered from different places

7. Where did you find the wasp? How did she act? Do you think that she can sting? How does she pass the winter?

8. Do you know the mud wasps which build the little, jug-shaped nests for their young? Do you know the mud wasps which utilize crevices and keyholes for their nests and plaster up the opening?

9. Do you know about the digger wasps which pack away grasshoppers or caterpillars in a hole in the ground, in which they lay their egg and then cover it?

Supplementary reading— Insect Stories, Kellogg; *Wasps, Social and Solitary*, Peckham; *Wasps and their Ways*, Morley; *The Ways of the Six-footed*, Comstock; *Home Studies in Nature*, Treat.

Fir0002/Flagstaffotos (GFDL v1.2)

The Yellow-Jacket

Teacher's Story

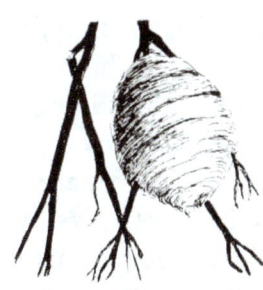

MANY wasps are not so waspish after all when we understand one important fact about them; i. e., although they are very nervous themselves, they detest that quality in others. For years the yellow-jackets have shared with us our meals at our summer camp on the lake shore. They make inquisitive tours of inspection over the viands on the table, often seeming to include ourselves, and coming so near that they fan our faces with their wings. They usually end by selecting the sweetened fruits, but they also carry off bits of roast beef, pouncing down upon the meat platter and seizing a tidbit as a hawk does a chicken. We always remain calm during these visitations, for we know that unless we inadvertently pinch one, we shall not be harmed; and it is great fun to watch one of these graceful creatures poising daintily on the side of the dish lapping up the fruit juice as a cat does milk, the slender, yellow-banded abdomen palpitating as she breathes. Occasionally, two desire the same place, and a wrestling match ensues which is fierce while it lasts, but the participants always come back to the dish unharmed. They are extra polite

A yellow-jacket

in their manners, for after one has delved eagerly into the fruit syrup, she proceeds to clean her front feet by passing them through her jaws, which is a wasp way of using a finger bowl.

Both yellow-jackets and the white-faced black-hornets build in trees and similarly, although the paper made by the yellow-jackets is finer in texture. However, some species of yellow-jackets build their nests in the ground, but of similar form. The nest is of paper made of bits of wood which the wasps pull off with their jaws from weather-worn fences or boards. This wood is reduced to a pulp by saliva which is secreted from the wasp's mouth, and is laid on in little layers which can be easily seen by examining the outside of the nest. These layers may be of different colors. A wasp will come with her load of paper pulp, and using her jaws and front feet for tools she will join a strip to the edge of the paper and pat it into shape. The paper tears more readily along the lines of the joining, than across. The cover of the nest is made of many layers of shell-like pieces fastened together and the outer layers are waterproof; the opening of a nest is at the bottom. Mr. Lubbock has shown that certain wasps are stationed at the door, as sentinels, to give warning on the approach of the enemy. The number of stories of combs in a nest depends upon the age and size of the colony. They are fastened together firmly near the center, by a central core or axis of very strong, firm paper, which at the top is attached to a branch or whatever supports the nest. The cells all open downward, in this respect differing from those of the honey-bee, which are usually placed horizontal. The wasp-comb differs from the honey-comb in that it is made of paper instead of wax, and that the rows of cells are single instead of double. The cells in the wasp-comb are not for storing honey, but are simply the cradles for the young wasps.

Sometimes a wasp family disaster makes it possible for us to examine one of these nests with its inmates. Here we find in some of the cells, the long white eggs fastened to the very bottom of the cell, in an inner angle, as if a larva when hatched needed to have a cozy corner. These wasp larvae are the chubbiest little grubs imaginable and are very soft bodied. It was once a mystery to me how they were able to hang in the cells, head down, without getting "black in the face" or falling out; but

OPO TERSER (CC BY 2.0)
Looking a wasp in the face

this was made plain by studying the little disk at the rear end of the larva's body, which is decidedly sticky; after a larva is dead, its heavy body can be lifted by pressing a match against this disk; thus it evidently suffices to keep the baby wasp stuck fast to its cradle. The larva's body is mostly covered with a white, papery, soft skeleton skin; the head is yellowish and highly polished, looking like a drop of honey. At one side may be seen a pair of toothed jaws, showing that it is able to take and chew any food brought by the nurses. They seem to be well trained youngsters for they all face toward the center of the nest, so that a nurse, when feeding them, can move from one to another without having to pass to the other side of the cell. It is a funny sight to behold a combful of well grown larvae, each fitting in its cell like meal in a bag and with head and several segments projecting out as if the bag were overflowing. It behooves the wasp larva to get its head as far out of the cell as possible, so that it will not be overlooked by the nurses; the little ones do this by holding themselves at the angle of the cell; this they accomplish by wedging the back into the corner. These young larvae do not face inwards like the older ones, but they rest in an inner angle of the cell.

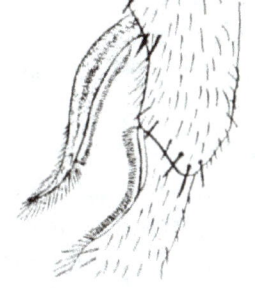

The antenna-comb on the wrist of my Lady Wasp

After a larva has reached the limit of its cell room, it spins a veil

Hornetboy1970 (cc by-sa 3.0)

around itself and fastens it at the sides, so that it forms a lining to the upper part of the cell and makes a bag over the "head and shoulders" of the insect. This cocoon is very tough, and beneath its loose dome the larva skin is shed; the pupa takes on a decidedly waspish form, except that the color is all black; the legs and the wings are folded piously down the breast and the antennae lie meekly each side of the face, with the "hands" folded outside of them; the strong toothed jaws are ready, so that when the pupa skin is molted, the insect can cut its silken curtain, and come out into its little nest world, as a full-fledged yellow-jacket.

What a harlequin the wasp is, in her costume of yellow and black! Often in the invertebrate world these colors mean "sit up and take notice," and the wasp's costume is no exception. Whoever has had any experience in meddling with yellow-jackets, avoids acquaintance with all yellow and black insects. Yet we must confess that the lady wasp has good taste in dress. The yellow cross bands on her black skirt are scalloped, and, in fact, all her yellow is put on in a most *chic* manner; she, being slender, can well afford to dress in roundwise stripes, and she folds her wings prettily like a fan, and not over her back like the mud wasp, which would cover her decorations. There is a sensation coming to the one who, armed with a lens, looks a wasp in the face; she always does her hair pompadour, and the yellow is here put on with a most bizarre effect, in points and arabesques. Even her jaws are yellow with black borders and black notches. Her antennae are velvety black, her legs are yellow, and her antennae comb, on her wrist, is a real comb and quite ornate.

In the nest which we studied in late August, the queen cells were just being developed. They were placed in a story all by themselves, and they were a third larger than the cells of the workers. The queen of this nest was a most majestic wasp, fully twice as large as any of her subjects; her face was entirely black, and the yellow bands on her long abdomen were of quite a different pattern than those on the workers; her sting was not so long in proportion, but I must confess it looked efficient. In fact, a yellow-jacket's sting is a formidable looking spear when seen through a microscope, since it has on one side some backward projecting barbs, meant to hold it firm when driving home the thrust.

While wasps are fond of honey and other sweets, they are also fond of animal food and eat a great many insects, benefiting us greatly by destroying mosquitoes and flies. As no food is stored for their winter use, all wasps excepting the queens die of the cold. The queens crawl away to protected places and seem to be able to withstand the rigors of winter; each queen, in the spring, makes a little comb of a few cells, covering it with a thin layer of paper. She then lays eggs in these cells and gathers food for the young; but when these first members of the family, which are always workers, come to maturity, they take upon themselves the work of enlarging the nest and caring for the young. After that, the queen devotes her energies to laying eggs.

Wasps enlarge their houses by cutting away the paper from the in-

side of the covering, to give more room for building the combs wider; to compensate for this, they build additional layers on the outside of the nest. Thus it is, that every wasp's nest, however large, began as a little comb of a few cells and was enlarged to meet the needs of the rapidly growing family. Ordinarily the nest made one year is not used again.

Lesson

Leading thought— The wasps were the original paper makers, using wood pulp for the purpose. Some species construct their houses of paper in the trees or bushes while others build in the ground.

Method— Take a deserted wasp-nest, the larger the better, with sharp scissors remove one side of the covering of the nest, leaving the combs exposed and follow with the questions and suggestions indicated. From this study of the nest encourage the children to observe more closely the wasps and their habits, which they can do in safety if they learn to move quietly while observing.

Observations—

1. Which kind of wasp do you think made this nest? Of what is the nest made? Where did the wasp get the material? How do the wasps make wood into paper?

2. What is the general shape of the nest? Is the nest well covered to protect it from rain? Where is the door where the wasps went in and out? Is the covering of the nest all of the same color? Do these differences in color give you any idea of how the wasps build the paper into the nest? Does the paper tear more easily one way than another? Is the covering of the nest solid or in layers?

3. How many combs or stories are there in the wasp house? How are they fastened together and how suspended?

4. Compare the combs of the wasp-nest with those of the honey-bee. How do they resemble each other and how differ? Do the cells open upward or downward? For what purpose are the combs in the wasp-nest used? Are all the cells of the same size? Do you know the reason for this difference in size?

5. How do the young wasp grubs manage to cling to the cells head downward? Are the cells lined with a different color and does this lining

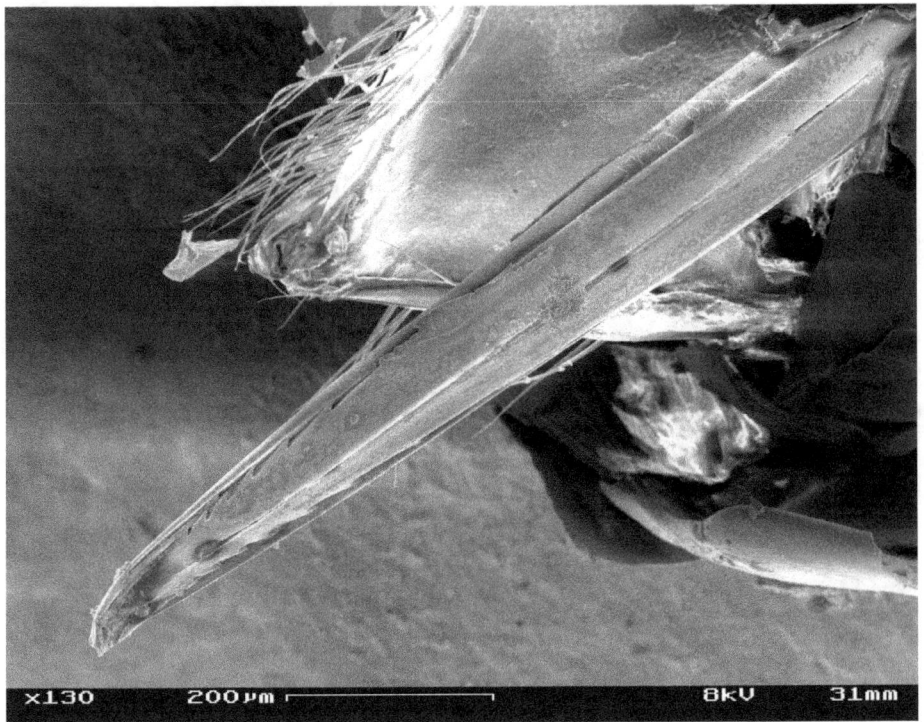
The greatly magnified sting of a yellow jacket in its sheath

extend out over the opening in some cases? Is this lining of the cells made of paper also? Do you know how a young wasp looks and how the white lining of the cells is made?

6. Do you believe that some wasps of the colony are always posted as sentinels at the door to give warning if the colony is attacked?

7. Do wasps store food to sustain them during the winter? What happens to them during winter? Is the same nest used year after year?

8. Can you describe the beginning of this wasp-nest? When was it made? Tell the story of the wasp that made it. How large was the nest at first? How was the nest enlarged?

9. What is the food of wasps? How do these insects benefit us?

10. Write a story giving the life history of a wasp.

11. In the summer watch a yellow-jacket eat from a dish of sweetened fruit which you may place out of doors to coax her to come where you can carefully observe her. What are the colors of the yellow-jacket? Where is the yellow? How are the yellow bands made ornamental? How does she fold her wings? How many wings has she? What is the color of her legs? Describe her antennae and eyes. How does she eat the fruit juice? Can you see the motion of her body when she breathes?

IVAR LEIDUS (CC BY-SA 4.0)

A male Megachile *leaf cutter bee*

The Leaf-Cutter Bee

TEACHER'S STORY

ONE beautiful day in late June when I was picking some roses, I saw a bee, almost as large as a honey-bee but different in shape and darker in color, alight on a leaf and moving with nervous rapidity, cut a circle out of a leaf with her jaws "quicker'n a wink;" then taking the piece between her fore-feet and perhaps holding it also with her jaws, she flew away, the green disk looking as large in proportion to her size as a big base drum hung to the neck of a small drummer. I waited long for her to come back, but she came not; meanwhile I examined the leaves of the rose bush and found many circlets, and also many oblong holes with the ends deeply rounded, cut from the leaflets.

I knew the story of the little bee and was glad I had seen her cut a leaflet with her jaw shears, which work sidewise like real shears. I knew that somewhere she had found a cavity big enough for her needs;

perhaps she had tunneled it herself in the dead wood of some post or stump, using her jaws to cut away the chips; maybe she had found a crevice beneath the shingles of a roof or beneath a stone in the field, or she may have rolled a leaf; anyway, her little

BERNHARD PLANK (CC BY-SA 3.0)
Cutting a leaf

cave was several inches long, circular in outline and large enough to admit her body. She first cut a long piece from the rose leaf and folded it at the end of the tunnel; and then she brought another and another long piece and bent and shaped them into a little thimble-like cup, fastening them together with some saliva glue, from her mouth. After the cup was made to her liking, she went in search of food, which was found in the pollen of some flowers. This pollen was carried not as the honey-bees do, because she has no pollen baskets on her legs; but it was dusted into the fur on the lower side of her body; as she scraped the pollen off, she mixed it with some nectar which she had also found in the flowers, and made it into a pasty mass and heaped it at the bottom of the cup; she probably made many visits to flowers before she had a sufficient amount of this bee pastry, and then she laid an egg upon it; after this, she immediately flew back to the rose bush to cut a lid for her cup. She is a nice mathematician and she cuts the lid just a little larger than the rim of the cup, so that it may be pushed down in, making it fit very closely around the edges; she then cuts another and perhaps another of the same size and puts them over and fastened to the first cover. When finished, it is surely the prettiest baby basket ever made by a mother, all safely enclosed to keep out enemies. But her work is then only begun. She has other baby baskets to make and she perhaps makes ten or more, placing one cup just ahead of another in the little tunnel.

But what is happening meanwhile to the bee babies in the baskets?

Carrying a cut leaf — PJT56 (CC BY-SA 3.0)

The egg hatches into a little white bee grub which falls to and eats the pollen and nectar paste with great eagerness. As it eats, it grows and sheds its skeleton skin as often as it becomes too tight, and then eats and grows some more. How many mothers would know just how much food it would require to develop a child from infancy until it grows up! This bee mother knows well this amount and when the food is all gone, the little bee grub is old enough to change to a pupa; it looks very different now, and although mummy-shaped we can see its folded wings and antennae. After remaining a motionless pupa for a few days, it sheds its pupa skin and now it is a bee just like its mother; but as the oldest bee is at the bottom of the tunnel, even after it gets its wings and gnaws its way out of its basket, it very likely cannot escape and find its way out into the sunshiny world, until its younger brothers and sisters have gone out before it.

There are many species of these leaf-cutter bees and each species makes its own kind of a nest, always cutting the same size of circlets and usually choosing its own special kind of leaf to make this cradle. Some are daintier in their tastes and use rolled petals instead of leaves; and we have found some tiny cups made of gorgeous peony petals, and some of pansy petals, a most exquisite material.

At Chautauqua we found a species which rolled maple leaves into a tube which held three or four cups, and we also found there a bee stowing her cups in the open end of a tubular rod, used to hold up an

Subbu Subramanya (CC BY-SA 4.0)
Dissected nest of a Megachile *leaf cutter*

awning. There are other species which make short tunnels in the ground for their nests, but perhaps the most common of all wedge their cups between or beneath the shingles on the roofs of summer cottages. But, however or wherever the leaf-cutter works, she is a master mechanic and does her work with niceness and daintiness.

Lesson

Leading thought— When we see the edges of rose leaves with holes of regular pattern in them, some of the holes being oblong and some circular, we know the leaf-cutter bee has cut them to make her cradle cups.

Method— It is very easy to find in June or autumn the leaves from which the leaf-cutter bee has cut the bedding for her young. Encourage the pupils to look for the nest during the summer and to bring some of the cups to school when they return, where they may be studied in detail; meanwhile the teacher may tell the story of the nest. This is rather difficult for the pupils to work out.

Observations—

1. Do you find rose leaves with round holes cut in their edges? Do you find on the same bush some leaflets with oblong holes in them? Sketch or describe the rose leaf thus cut, noting exactly the shape of the holes. Are the circular holes of the same size? Are the long holes about equal in size and shape? Do you find any other plants with holes like these cut in them? Do you find any petals of flowers thus cut?

2. What do you think made these holes? If an insect was taking a leaf for food would the holes be as regular? Watch the rose bush carefully and see if you can discover the insect which cuts the leaf.

Pupa of a leafcutter bee

3. Have you ever seen the little black bee carrying pieces of rose leaves between her front feet? With what instrument do you suppose she cut the leaves? Where do you think she was going?

4. Have you ever found the nest of the leaf-cutter bee? Was it in a tunnel made in dead wood or in some crack or cranny? How many of the little rose leaf cups are there in it? How are the cups placed? Are the little bees still in the cups or can you see the holes through which they crawled out?

5. Take one cup and study it carefully. How are the pieces of leaves folded to make the cups? How is the lid put on? Soak the cup in water until it comes apart easily. Describe how many of the long pieces were used and how they were bent to make a cup. Of how many thicknesses is the cover made? Are the covers just the same size or a little larger than the top of the cup? How does the cover fit so tightly?

6. If you find the nest in July or early August, examine one of the cups carefully and see what there is in it. Take off the cover without injuring it. What is at the bottom of the nest? Is there an insect within it? How does it look? What is it doing? Of what do you think its food was made? How and by whom was the food placed in the cup? Place the nest in a box or jar with mosquito netting over the top, and put it out of doors in a safe and shaded place. Look at it often and see what this insect changes into.

7. If the mother bee made each little nest cup and put in the bee-bread, and honey for her young, which cup contains the oldest of the family? Which the youngest? How do you think the full-grown bees get out of the cup?

8. Do you think that the same species of bee always cuts the same sized holes in a leaf? Is it the same species which cuts the rose leaves and the pansy petals?

The Little Carpenter-Bee

TEACHER'S STORY

TAKE a dozen dead twigs from almost any sumac or elder, split them lengthwise, and you will find in at least one or two of them, a little tunnel down the center where the pith once was. In the month of June or July, this narrow tunnel is made into an insect apartment house, one little creature in each apartment, partitioned off from the one above and the one below. The nature of this partition reveals to us whether the occupants are bees or wasps; if it is made of tiny chips, like fine sawdust glued together, a bee made it and there are little bees in the cells; if it is made of bits of sand or mud glued together, a wasp was the architect and young wasps are the inhabitants. Also, if the food in the cells is pollen paste, it was placed there by a bee; if of paralyzed insects or spiders, a wasp made the nest.

The little carpenter-bee *(Ceratina dupla)* is a beautiful creature, scarcely one quarter of an inch in length, with metallic blue body and

Typical interior of a small carpenter bee's nest, this one is in a dry fennel stem. Notice the cells, each containing pollen bread and one offspring. The right larva has hatched

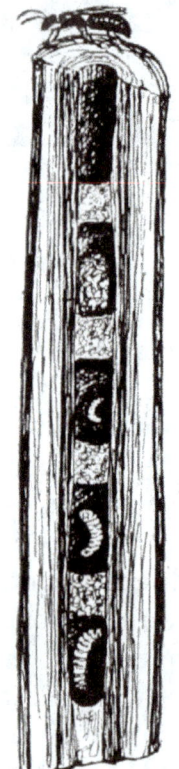

The little carpenter-bee; her nest, cut open, showing the eldest larva at the bottom and the youngest nearest the entrance

rainbow tinted wings. In May, she selects some broken twig of sumac, elder or raspberry, which gives her access to the pith; this she at once begins to dig out, mouthful by mouthful, until she has made a smooth tunnel several inches long; she then gathers pollen and packs bee-bread in the bottom of the cell to the depth of a quarter-inch, and then lays upon it, a tiny white egg. She then brings back some of her chips of pith and glues them together, making a partition about one-tenth of an inch thick, which she fastens firmly to the sides of the tunnel; this is the roof for the first cell and the floor of the next one; she then gathers more pollen, lays another egg, and builds another partition.

Thus she fills the tunnel, almost to the opening, with cells, sometimes as many as fourteen; but she always leaves a space for a vestibule near the door, and in this she makes her home while her family below her are growing up.

The egg in the lowest cell of course hatches first; a little bee grub issues from it and eats the bee-bread industriously and grows by shedding his skin when it becomes too tight; then he changes to a pupa and later to a bee resembling his mother. But, though fully grown, he cannot get out into the sunshine, for all his younger brothers and sisters are blocking the tunnel ahead of him; so he simply tears down the partition above him

Nest of carpenter-wasp

and kicks the little pieces of it behind him, and bides his time until the next youngest brother tears down the partition above his head and pushes its fragments behind him into the very face of the elder which, in turn, performs a similar act; and thus, while he is waiting, he is kept more or less busy pushing behind him the broken bits of all the partitions above him. Finally, the youngest gets his growth, and there they all are in the tunnel, the broken partitions behind the hindmost at the bottom of the nest, and the young bees packed closely together in a row with heads toward the door. When we find the nest at this period, we know the mother because her head is toward her young ones and her back to the door. A little later, on some bright morning, they all come out into the sunshine and flit about on gauzy, rainbow wings, a very happy family, out of prison.

But if the brood is a late one, the home must be cleaned out and used as a winter nest, and still the loyal little mother bee stays true to her post; she is the last one to enter the nest; and not until they are all housed within, does she enter. It is easy to distinguish her for her poor wings are torn and frayed with her long labor of building the nest, until they scarcely serve to carry her afield; but despite this she remains on guard over her brood, for which she has worn out her own life. The story of the little carpenter-wasps is similar to that of the bee, except that we have reason to believe they often use her abandoned tunnels instead of making new ones. They make their little partitions out of mud; their pupae are always in long, slender, silken cocoons, and we have no evidence that the mother remains in attendance.

LESSON

Leading thought— Not all bees live in colonies like the honey-bees and bumblebees. One tiny bee rears her brood within a tunnel which she makes in the pith of sumac, elder or raspberry.

Method— This lesson may be given in June or in October. In June, the whole family of bees in their apartments may be observed; in autumn, the empty tenement with the fragments of the partitions still clinging may be readily found and examined; and sometimes a whole family may be found, stowed away in the home tunnel, for the winter.

Observations—

1. Collect dead twigs of sumac or elder and cut them in half, lengthwise. Do you find any with the pith tunneled out?

2. How long is the tunnel? Are its sides smooth? Can you see the partitions which divide the long narrow tunnel into cells? Look at the partitions with a lens, if necessary, to determine whether they are made of tiny bits of wood or of mud. If made of mud, what insect made them? If of little chips how and by what were they constructed?

3. Are there any insects in the cells? If so, describe them. Is there bee-bread in the cells?

4. For what was the tunnel made? With what tools was it made? How are the partitions fastened together? How does a young bee look?

5. Write the story of the oldest of the bee family which lived in this tunnel. Why did it hatch first? On what did it feed? When it became a full fledged bee, what did it do? How did it finally get out?

6. Take a glass tube, the hollow at the center being about one-eighth of an inch across, a tube which you can get in any drug-store. Break this tube into sections, six or seven inches long, wrap around each a black paper or cloth, made fast with rubber bands and suspend them in a hedge or among thick bushes in May. Examine these tubes each week to see if the wasps or bees are using them.

Nest of large carpenter-bee

Supplementary reading— "The Story We Love Best," in *Ways of the Six-footed*, Comstock.

Angella Moorehouse (cc by-sa 4.0)
Female (left) and male (right) bumblebees

The Bumblebee

Teacher's Story

*Thou, in sunny solitudes,
Rover of the underwoods,
The green silence dost replace
With thy mellow, breezy bass.*

—Emerson.

HERE seems to have been an hereditary war between the farm boy and the bumblebee, the hostilities usually initiated by the boy. Like many wars, it is very foolish and wicked, and has resulted in great harm to both parties. Luckily, the boys of to-day are more enlightened; and it is to be hoped that they will learn to endure a bee sting or two for the sake of protecting these diminishing hosts, upon which so many flowers depend for carrying their pollen; for of all the insects of the field, the bumblebees are the best and most needed friends of the flowers.

The bumblebees are not so thrifty and forehanded as are the honey-bees, and do not provide enough honey to sustain the whole colony during the winter. Only the mother bees, or queens as they are called, survive the cold season. Just how they do it, we do not know, but probably they are better nourished and therefore have more endurance than the workers. In early May, one of the most delightful of

Phelyan Sanjoin (CC by-sa .0)

Red-tailed bumblebee nest. Notice the full honey pots

spring visitors is one of these great buzzing queens, flying low over the freshening meadows, trying to find a suitable place for her nest; and the farmer or fruit grower who knows his business, is as anxious as she that she find suitable quarters, knowing well that she and her children will render him most efficient aid in growing his fruit and seed. She finally selects some cosy place, very likely a deserted nest of the field mouse, and there begins to build her home. She toils early and late, gathering pollen and nectar from the blossoms of the orchard and other flowers which she mixes into a loaf as large as a bean upon which she lays a few tiny eggs and then covers with wax. She then makes a honey-pot of wax as large as a small thimble and fills it with honey; thus provided with food she broods over her eggs, keeping them warm until they hatch. Each little bee grub then burrows into the bee-bread making for itself a cave while satisfying its hunger. When fully grown, it spins about itself a cocoon, changes to a pupa and then comes out a true bumblebee but smaller than her queen mother. These workers are daughters and are happy in caring for the growing family; they gather pollen and nectar and add to the mass of bee-bread for the young to burrow in, meanwhile the queen remains at home and devotes her energies to laying eggs. The workers not only care for the young, but later they strengthen the silken pupa cradles with wax, and thus make them into cells for storing honey. When we understand that the cells in the bumblebee's nest are simply made by the young bees burrowing in any direction, we can understand why the bumblebee comb is so disorderly in the arrangement of its cells.

CERIDWEN (CC BY-SA 2.0)
This bumblebee nest has been raided

Perhaps the boy of the farm would find the rank bumblebee honey less like the ambrosia of the gods if he knew that it was stored in the deserted cradles and swaddling clothes of the bumblebee grubs.

All of the eggs in the bumblebee nest in the spring and early summer develop into workers which do incidentally the vast labor of carrying pollen for thousands of flowers; to these only is granted the privilege of carrying the pollen for the red clover, since the tongues of the other bees are not sufficiently long to reach the nectar. The red clover does not produce seed in sufficient quantity to be a profitable crop, unless there are bumblebees to pollinate its blossoms. Late in the summer, queens and drones are developed in the bumblebee nest, the drones, as with the honey-bees, being mates for the queens. But of all the numerous population of the bumblebee nest, only the queens survive the rigors of winter, and on them and their success depends the future of the bumblebee species.

There are many species of bumblebees, some much smaller than others, but they all have the thorax covered with plush above and the abdomen hairy, and their fur is usually marked in various patterns of pale yellow and black. The bumblebee of whatever species, has short but very active antennae and a mouth fitted for biting as well as for sucking. Between the large compound eyes are three simple eyes. The wings are four in number and strong; the front legs are very short; all the legs have hairs over them and end in a three-jointed foot, tipped by a claw. On the hind leg, the tibia and the first tarsal joint are enlarged, making the pollen baskets on which the pollen is heaped in

Bumblebee in flight. It has its tongue extended and a laden pollen basket

golden masses. One of the most interesting observations possible to make, is to note how the bumblebee brushes the pollen from her fur and packs it into her pollen baskets.

Lesson

Leading thought— The bumblebees are the chief pollen carriers for most of our wild flowers as well as for the clovers and other farm plants. They should, therefore, be kindly treated everywhere; and we should be careful not to hurt the big queen bumblebee which we see often in May.

Method— Ask the questions and encourage the pupils to answer them as they have opportunity to observe the bumblebees working in the flowers. A bumblebee may be imprisoned in a tumbler for a short period for observation, and then allowed to go unharmed. It is not advisable to study the nest, which is not only a dangerous proceeding for the pupil, but it also means the destruction of a colony of these very useful insects. However, if the location of a nest is discovered, it may be dug up and studied after the first heavy frost. Special stress should be laid upon the observations of the actions of the bees when visiting flowers.

Observations—

1. In how many flowers do you find the bumblebee? Watch her closely and see how she gets the nectar. Notice how she "bumbles around" in a flower and becomes dusted with pollen. Watch her

Pahazzard (cc by-sa 3.0)
Using its tongue to drink nectar

and note how she gets the pollen off her fur and packs it in her pollen baskets. On which legs are her pollen baskets? How does the pollen look when packed in them? What does she do with pollen and nectar?

2. Catch a bumblebee in a jelly glass and look at her closely. Can you see three little eyes between the big compound eyes? Describe her antennae. Are they active? How many pairs of wings has she? Do you think they are strong? Which pair of legs is the shortest? How many segments are there in the leg? Do you see the claws on the foot?

3. What is the bumblebee's covering? What is the color of her plush? Is she furry above and below?

4. Can you see that she can bite as well as suck with her mouthparts? Will a bumblebee sting a person unless she is first attacked?

5. Have you seen the very large queen bumblebee in the spring, flying near the ground hunting for a place to build a nest? Why must you be very careful not to hurt her? How does she pass the winter? What does she do first, in starting the nest?

6. In how many ways does the bumblebee benefit us?

Foragers loaded with pollen on the hive landing board

The Honey-Bee

TEACHER'S STORY

URING many years naturalists have been studying the habits and adaptations of the honey-bees, and, as yet, the story of their wonderful ways is not half told. Although we know fairly well what the bees do, yet we have no inkling of the processes which lead to a perfect government and management of the bee community; and even the beginner may discover things never known before about these fascinating little workers. In beginning this work it might be well to ask the pupils if they have ever heard of a republic that has many kings and only one queen; and where the citizens do all the governing without voting, and where the kings are powerless and the queen works as hard and longer than any of her subjects; and then tell them that the pages of history contain no account of a republic so wonderful as this; yet the nearest beehive is the home of just this sort of government.

In addition to the interest of the bee colony from a nature-study stand-point, it is well to get the children interested in bee-keeping as a commercial enterprise. A small apiary well managed may bring in an acceptable income; and it should be the source of a regular revenue to the boys and girls of the farm, for one hive should net the young bee-keeper from three to five dollars per year and prove a business education to him in the meantime.

Bees are perfect socialists. They have non-competitive labor, united capital, communal habitations and unity of interests. The

An africanized honey bee (left) and a European honey bee (right)

bee commune is composed of castes as immutable as those of the Brahmins, but these castes exist for the benefit of the whole society instead of for the individuals belonging to them. These castes we have named queens, drones and workers, and perhaps, first of all, we should study the physical adaptations of the members of these castes for their special work in the community.

THE WORKER

There are three divisions to the body of the bee, as in all insects—head, thorax and abdomen. The head bears the eyes, antennae and mouth-parts, (p. 214, W.) There are two large compound eyes on either side of the head and three simple eyes between them. The antennae arise from the face, each consisting of two parts, one straight segment at the base, and the end portion which is curved and made up of many segments. There is also a short, bead-like segment where the antenna joins the face. A lens is needed to see the jaws of the bee, folded across, much like a pair of hooks, and below them the tongue, which is a sucking tube; the length of the tongue is very important, for upon this depends the ability of the bee to get nectar from the flowers.

The thorax bears three pairs of legs below and two pairs of wings above. Each leg consists of six segments, and the foot or tarsus has

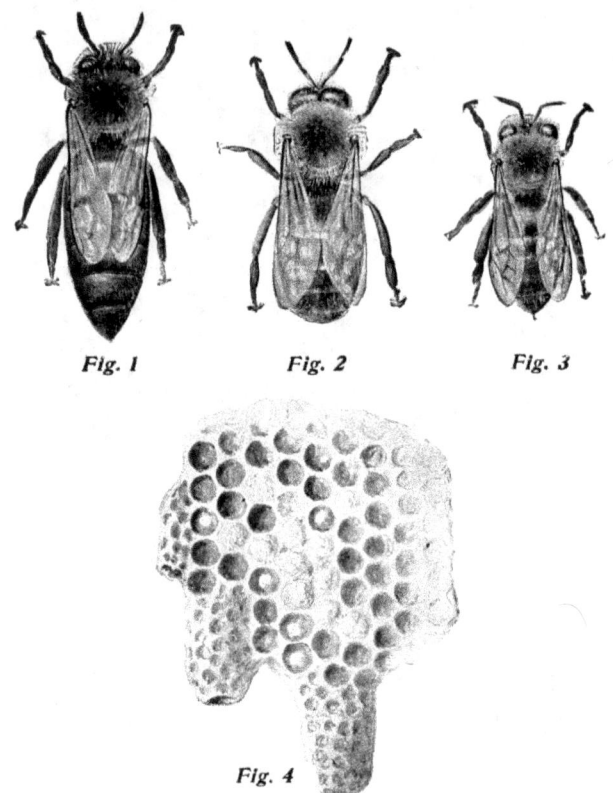

Fig. 1   *Fig. 2*   *Fig. 3*

Fig. 4

1. Queen bee; 2. Drone; 3. Worker; all enlarged; 4. Queen cells.

four segments and a pair of claws. The front leg has an antennae comb between the tibia and tarsus, (p. 213, F, a,) the hind leg has a pollen basket, which is a long cavity bordered by hairs wherein the pollen is packed and carried (p. 213, A, pb.) On the other side of the large joint beyond the pollen basket are rows of spines which are used to remove the pollen from the baskets (p. 213, B, pc,) and between these two large segments are the pincers for removing the wax (p. 213, B, wp.)

The front pair of wings is larger than the hind pair. The wings of the old bees that have done much work are always frayed at the edges.

There are six segments or rings to the abdomen, plainly visible from above. If the five segments next the thorax are marked above with yellow bands on their front edges, the bee is an Italian. On the lower side of the abdomen, each segment is made up of a central plate with an over-lapping plate on each side; just at the front edge on each

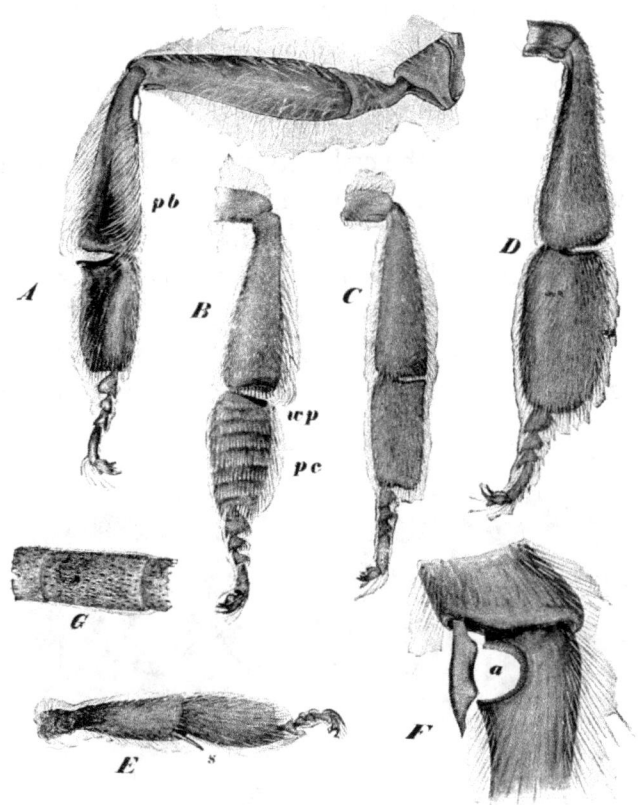

Legs of worker honey-bee.
A, outer surface of hind leg showing the nine segments and claws; pb, the pollen basket of tibia; B, inner surface of part of hind leg; wp, wax-pincers; pc, pollen-combs; C, inner surface of part of hind leg of queen; D, inner surface of part of hind leg of drone; E, part of middle leg of worker; s, spur; F, part of fore leg showing the antenna cleaner a; G, part of antenna showing sense-hairs and sense-pits.

side of the central plate is a wax pocket which cannot be seen unless the bee is dissected under a microscope. From these pockets are secreted little flecks of wax (p. 214, X.)

THE QUEEN

The queen bee is a truly royal insect. She is much larger than the worker, her body being long, pointed, and extending far beyond the tips of her closed wings, giving her a graceful form. She has no pollen baskets or pollen comb upon her legs, because it is not a part of her work to gather pollen or honey. The queen bee starts life as an ordinary worker egg, which is selected for special development. The workers tear down the partitions of the cells around the chosen egg and build a projection over the top, making an apartment, (p. 212, Fig. 4.) The little white bee grub, as soon as it hatches, is fed for five days on the same food as is given to the worker grubs for three days; it is a special substance, secreted by the worker bees, called royal jelly. This food is very nourishing, and after being reared upon it, the princess larva weaves around herself a silken cocoon and changes to a pupa. Meanwhile the

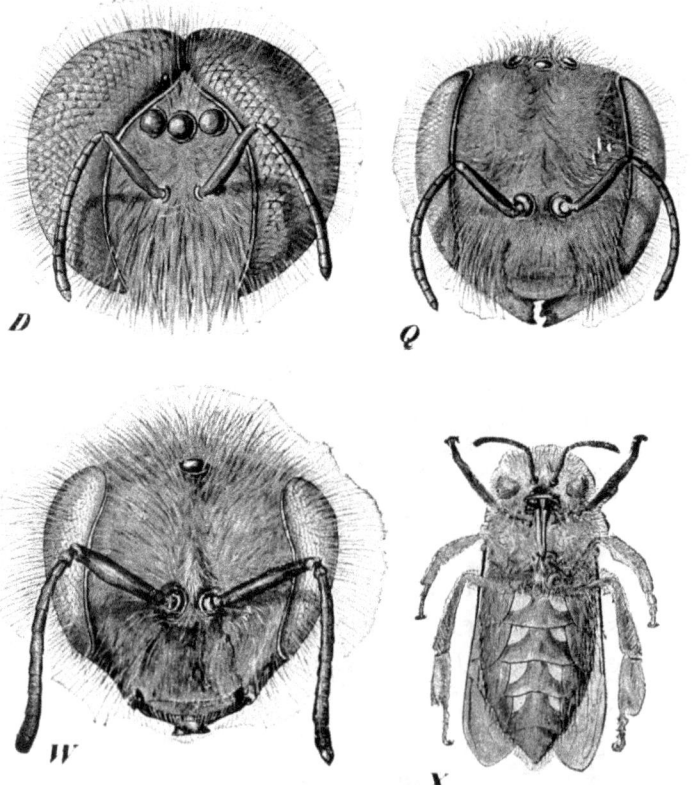

D, head of drone; Q, head of queen bee; W, head of worker; X, worker bee seen from below, showing plates of wax secreted from wax pockets.

workers have sealed her cell with wax.

When the princess-pupa changes to the full-grown queen she cuts a circular door in the cover of the cell and pushes through it into the world. Her first real work is to hunt for other queen cells and if she finds one, she will, if not hindered, make a hole in its side and sting to death the poor princess within. If she finds another full-grown queen, the two fight until one succumbs. The queen never uses her sting upon anything or anyone except a rival queen.

JESSICA LAWRENCE (CC BY 3.0)
A queen bee with workers

After a few days she takes her marriage flight in the air, where she mates with some drone, and then returns to her hive and begins her great work as mother of the colony. She runs about on the comb, pokes her head into a cell to see if it is ready, then turning about thrusts her abdomen in and neatly glues an egg fast to the bottom.

When the honey season is at its height she works with great rapidity, sometimes laying at the rate of six eggs per minute, often producing 3,000 eggs during a day, which would equal twice her own weight. If the workers do not allow her to destroy the other queens, she then takes a portion of her colony with her and swarms out, seeking a home elsewhere.

THE DRONE

The drone differs much in shape from the queen and the worker. He is broad and blunt, being very different in shape from the queen, and larger than the worker, (p. 212, Fig. 2.) He has no pollen baskets on his legs and has no sting. His eyes are very much larger than those of the queen or the worker and unite at the top of the head (p. 214, D.) His wings are larger and stronger than those of the worker or queen. It is not his business to go out and gather honey or to help in the work of the hive. His tongue is not long enough to get honey from the flowers; he has no pollen basket in which to carry pollen; he has no sting to fight enemies and no pockets for secreting wax; he is fed by his sister workers until the latter part of the season when the honey supply runs low, and then he is stung or bitten to death by these same sisters who have always given him such good care. The drone should be called a prince or king, since his particular office in the hive is to mate with the queen.

References— *How to Keep Bees*, Comstock; *The Bee People*, Morley.

WAUGSBERG (CC BY-SA 3.0)
Honeycomb with eggs

WAUGSBERG (CC BY-SA 3.0)
3-4 day old larvae

WAUGSBERG (CC BY-SA 3.0)
The development of a drone pupa

WAUGSBERG (CC BY-SA 3.0)
Drone pupae. The ones on the right are older

The birth of a honey bee

LESSON

Leading thought— In a colony of honey-bees there are three different forms of bees, the queens, the drones, and the workers. All of these have their own special work to do for the community.

Method— In almost every country or village community there is an apiary, or at least someone who keeps a few colonies of bees; to such the teacher must turn for material for this lesson. If this is not practical the teacher may purchase specimens from any bee dealer; she may, for instance, get an untested queen with attendant workers in a queen cage sent by mail for a small sum. These could be kept alive for some time by feeding them with honey, during which time the pupils can study the forms of the two castes. Any apiary during September will give enough dead drones for a class to observe. Although ordinarily we do not advocate the study of dead specimens, yet common sense surely has its place in nature-study; and in the case of the honey-bee, a closer study of the form of the insect is desirable than the living bee might see fit to permit. There are no more wonderful instances of adaptation of form to life than is found in the anatomy of the workers, queens and drones; moreover, it is highly desirable if the pupils are ever to become bee-keepers, that they shall know these adaptations.

A lens is almost necessary for these lessons and a compound microscope used with a low power would be a very desirable adjunct. This lesson should not be given below the fifth grade; and it is better adapted to eighth grade work.

The Worker

Observations—

1. How many divisions of the body are there?
2. What organs are borne on the head?
3. Are there small, simple eyes between the large compound ones?
4. What is the difference between the large eyes and the small?
5. Describe the antennae.
6. What can you see of the mouth? Describe it.
7. Look at the tongue under the microscope and see how it is fitted for getting nectar from flowers.
8. What organs are borne on the thorax?
9. Study the front or middle leg. How many joints has it?
10. With a lens find the antennae cleaner on the front leg. Describe it.
11. Describe the feet and claws.
12. Compare the third segment of the hind leg with that of the front leg.
13. Note that this segment of the hind leg is much wider. Note its form and describe how it forms the pollen basket.
14. Study the next segment of the hind leg, and note the wax pincers and the pollen combs.
15. Compare the front and hind wing as to shape and size.
16. How many rings are there on the abdomen and how are the rings colored above?
17. Study the lower side of the body; do you know where the wax comes from?
18. Write an English theme on the development of the larva of the worker bee; the duties of a worker bee from the time it issues from its cocoon until it dies working for the colony.

The Queen Bee

1. How does the queen differ in size and shape from the worker?
2. Has she pollen baskets or pollen combs on her hind legs?
3. How does the shape of the abdomen differ from that of the worker?

Collecting pollen

4. Write an English theme on the life of a queen bee. This should cover the following points: The kind of cell in which the queen is developed; the kind of food on which she is reared; the fact that she never stings people but reserves her sting for other queens; why she does not go out to gather honey; how and by whom and on what she is fed; she would not use pollen baskets if she had them; the work she does for the colony; the length of her life compared with that of a worker; the time of year when new queens are developed, and what becomes of the old queen when a new one takes her place; why she is called a queen.

THE DRONE

1. How does the drone differ in size and form of body from the worker?
2. How does he differ in these respects from the queen?
3. Has he pollen baskets on his legs?
4. Has he a sting?
5. Compare his eyes with those of the queen and worker.
6. Compare the size of his wings with those of the queen and worker.
7. Write an English theme on the drone. This should cover the following points: In what sort of cell is the drone developed; does he go out to gather honey or help in the work of the hive; how he is fed; how he is unfitted for work for the colony in the following particulars: Tongue, lack of pollen baskets, lack of sting, and of wax pockets; why the drone should be called a prince or king; the death of the drones; when and by what means it occurs.

The Honey-Comb

Teacher's Story

HE structure of honey-comb has been for ages admired by mathematicians, who have measured the angles of the cells and demonstrated the accurate manner in which the rhomb-shaped cell changes at its base to a three faced pyramid; and proven that, considering the material of construction, honey-comb exemplifies the strongest and most economic structure possible for the storing of liquid contents. While recent instruments of greater precision in measuring angles, show less perfection in honey-comb than the ancients believed, yet the fact still stands that the general plan of it is mathematically excellent.

Some have tried to detract from bee skill, by stating that the six-sided cell is simply the result of crowding cells together. Perhaps this was the remote origin of the hexagonal cell; but if we watch a bee build her comb, we find that she begins with a base laid out in triangular pyramids, on either side of which she builds out six-sided cells. A cell just begun, is as distinctly six-sided as when completed.

The shape of the cell of a honey-comb is six-sided in cross section. The bottom is a three-sided pyramid and its sides help form pyramids at the bottom of the cells opposite, thus economizing every particle of space. In the hive, the cells lie horizontal usually, although sometimes the combs are twisted. The honey is retained in the cell by a cap of wax which is made in a very cunning fashion; it consists of a circular disc at the middle supported from the six angles of the cell by six tiny girders. The comb is made fast to the section of the hive by being plastered upon it. The foundation comb sold to apiarists is quite thick, so that the edges of the cell may be drawn out and almost complete the sides of the cell. However, the foundation comb is expensive and is ordinarily used by the bee-keeper simply as a starter, which means a little strip a few inches or so in width fastened to the top of a section just to give the bees a hint that this is the direction in which the comb should be built, a hint which the bees invariably take. The cells of honey-comb are used also for the storing of bee-bread and also as cradles for the young bees.

A frame of honey. Note the caps to the cells, each supported by six girders

References— *The Bee People*, Morley; *How to Keep Bees*, Comstock.

Lesson

Leading thought— The cells of honey-comb are six-sided and in double rows and are very perfectly arranged for the storing of honey, so as to save room.

Materials— A section filled with honey and also a bit of empty comb

MUHAMMAD MAHDI KARIM (GFDL 1.2)
Honeycomb in a natural honey bee hive

and a bit of commercial foundation comb which may be obtained in any apiary.

Observations—

1. Look at a bit of empty honey-comb; what is the shape of the cell as you look down into it?

2. What is the shape of the bottom of the cell?

3. How does the bottom of the cell join the bottom of the cell opposite? Explain how honey-comb economizes space as storage for honey, and why an economy of space is of use to bees in the wild state.

4. In the hive is the honey-comb placed so that the length of the cells are horizontal or up and down?

5. Observe honey-comb containing honey; how is the honey retained in the cells?

6. Carefully take off a cap from the honey cell and see if you can find the six girders that extend inward from the angles of the cell to support the circular portion in the center.

7. By what means is the honey-comb made fast to the sides of the section or the hive?

8. Study a bit of foundation comb and note where the bees will pull out the wax to form the cell.

9. Why and how is foundation comb used by the bee-keeper?

10. For what purpose besides storing honey are the cells of honey-comb used by the bees?

Industries of the Hive and the Observation Hive

TEACHER'S STORY

BEE-HIVES are the houses which man furnishes for the bee colonies, the wild bees ordinarily living in hollow trees or in caves. The usual hive consists of a box which is the lower story and of one or more upper stories, called "supers." In the lower story are placed frames for the brood and for storing the honey for the winter use of the bees. In the supers are placed the sections, each of which is planned to hold a pound of honey. It is the habit of the bees to place their brood in the lower part of their nests and store honey in the upper portions. The bee-keepers have taken advantage of this habit of the bees and remove the supers with their filled sections and replace them with others to be filled, and thus get a large crop of honey. The number of bees in a colony varies; there should be at least 40,000 in a healthy colony. Of these a large proportion are workers; there may be a few hundred drones the latter part of the season but only one queen.

Honey-comb is built of wax and is hung from the frame so that the cells are horizontal; its purpose is to cradle the young and for the storage of pollen and honey. The wax used for building the comb is a secretion of the bees; when comb is needed, a number of self-elected bee citizens gorge themselves with honey and hang themselves up in a curtain, each bee reaching up with her fore feet and taking hold of the hind feet of the one above her. After remaining thus for some time the wax appears in little plates, one on each side of the second, third, fourth and fifth segments of the abdomen. This wax is chewed by the bees and made into comb.

Honey is made from the nectar of flowers which the bee takes into her honey stomach. This, by the way, is not the true stomach of the bee and has nothing to do with digestion. It is simply a receptacle for storing the nectar, which is mixed with some secretion from the glands of the bee which brings about chemical changes, the chief of which is changing the cane sugar of the nectar into the more easily digested grape sugar of the honey. After the honey is emptied from the honey stomach into the cell, it remains exposed to the air for some time before the cell is capped, and thus ripens. It is an interesting fact that up to the seventeenth century honey was the only means people had for sweetening their food, as sugar was unknown.

Bee-bread is made from the pollen of flowers which is perhaps mixed with saliva so as to hold together; it is carried from the field on the pollen baskets of the hind legs of the workers; it is packed into the cell by the bees and is used for food. Propolis is bee glue; it is used as a cement and varnish; it is gathered by the bees from the leaf-buds of certain trees and plants, although when they can get it, the bees will take fresh varnish. It is used as a filler to make smooth the rough places of the hive; it often helps hold the combs in place; it calks every crack; it is applied as a varnish to the cells of the honey-comb if they remain unused for a time, and if the door of the observation hive be left open the bees will cover the inside of the glass with this glue, and thus make the interior of the hive dark.

The young bees are footless, white grubs. Each one lives in its own little cell and is fed by the nurse bees, which give it partly digested food from their own stomachs.

The removal of honey from the supers does not do any harm to

The queen bee has been marked by the keeper for easy identification

the bee colony if there is enough honey left in the brood chambers to support the bees during the winter. There should be twenty-five or thirty pounds of honey left in the brood chamber for winter use. In winter, the hives should be protected from the cold by being placed in special houses or by being encased in larger boxes, leaving an opening so that the bees may come out in good weather. The chaff hive is best for both winter and summer, as it surrounds the hive with a space, which is filled with chaff, and keeps the hive warm in winter and cool in summer. Many bee-keepers put their bees in cellars during the winter, but this method is not as safe as the chaff hive. Care should be taken in summer to place the hives so that they are shaded at least part of the day. The grass should be mown around the hives so that the bees will not become entangled in it as they return from the fields laden with honey.

What may be seen in the observation hive— First of all, it is very interesting to watch the bees build their comb. When more comb is needed certain members of the colony gorge themselves with honey and remain suspended while it oozes out of the wax pockets on the lower side of the abdomen. This wax is collected and chewed to make it less brittle and then is carried to the place where the comb is being built and is molded into shape by the jaws of the workers. However, the bee that puts the wax in place is not always the one that molds it into comb.

A bee comes into the hive with her honey stomach filled with nectar and disgorges this into a cell. When a bee comes in loaded with pollen, she first brushes it from the pollen baskets on her hind legs

into the cell; later another worker comes along and packs the pollen grains into the cell with her head, which is a comical sight.

The bee nurses run about on the comb feeding the young bee grubs partially digested honey and pollen regurgitated from their own stomachs. Whenever the queen moves about the comb she is followed by a retinue of devoted attendants which feed her on the rich and perfectly digested royal jelly and also take care of her royal person and give her every attention possible. The queen, when laying, thrusts her abdomen into the cell and glues a little white egg to the bottom. The specially interesting thing about this is that the queen always lays an egg which will produce a female, or worker in the smaller cells and will always lay an egg to produce a drone or male in the larger cells.

If there is any foreign substance in the observation hive it is interesting to see the bees go to work at once to remove it. They dump all of the debris out in front of the hive. They close all crevices in the hive; and they will always curtain the glass, if the door is kept open too much, with propolis or bee glue, which is a very sticky substance which they get from leaf buds and other vegetable sources. When bees fan to set up a current of air in the hive, they glide back and forth, moving the wings so rapidly that we can only see a blur about their bodies.

If drones are developed in the hive, it is interesting to see how tenderly they are fed by their sister workers, although they do not hesitate to help themselves to the honey stored in the cells; and if the observation hive is working during September, undoubtedly the pupils may be able to see the murder of the drones by their sisters. But the children should understand that this killing of the drones is necessary for the preservation of the colony, as the workers cannot store enough honey to keep the colony alive during the winter if the drones were allowed to go on feeding.

If you see the worker bees fighting, it means that robbers are attempting to get at the stores of the observation hive. The entrance to the hive should at once be contracted by placing a block of wood in front, so that there is room for only one bee at a time to pass in and out.

Lesson

Leading thought— In the hive are carried on the industries of wax-making, building of honey-comb, storing of honey and bee-bread, caring for the young, keeping the hive clean and ventilated and calking all crevices with bee glue.

Method— This lesson should be in the nature of a demonstration. If there is an apiary in the neighborhood, it is quite possible that the teacher may show the pupils a hive ready for occupancy by the bees; in any case she will have no difficulty in borrowing a frame of brood comb, and this with a section of honey which can be bought at the grocery store, is sufficient if there is no observation hive. This lesson should be an informal talk between teacher and pupils.

An observation

The bees begin to build the comb from the top of each section. When a cell is filled with honey, the bees seal it with wax

hive in the schoolroom is an object of greatest interest to the pupils, as through its glass sides they may be able to verify for themselves the wonderful tales concerning the lives and doings of the bees which have been told us by naturalists. Moreover, the study thus made of the habits of the bees is an excellent preparation for the practical apiarist, and we sincerely believe that bee-keeping is one of the ways by which the boys and girls of the farm may obtain money for their own use.

The observation hive is very simply constructed and can be made by anyone who knows how to use ordinary carpenter tools. It is simply a small, ordinary hive with a pane of glass on each side which is covered by a hinged door. A hive thus made is placed so that the front end rests upon a window sill; the sash is lifted an inch or so, a strip of wood, or a piece of wire netting being inserted underneath the sash except in front of the entrance of the hive, to hinder the bees from coming back into the room. A covered passageway should extend from the entrance of the hive to the outside of the window sill. This window should be one which opens away from the playground so that the bees coming and going, will not come into collision with the pupils. The observation window should be kept carefully shut, except when the pupils are using it, since the bees object to light in their homes.

The A. I. Root Co., of Medina, Ohio, sell a pretty observation hive

Muhammad Mahdi Karim (GFDL 1.2)
A honey bee carrying pollen back to the hive

which we have used successfully by stocking it afresh each season, it being too small for a self-sustaining colony. But it has the advantage of smallness which enables us to see all that is going on within it, which would be impossible in a larger hive. This hive comes in several sizes, and will be shipped from the makers stocked with bees at prices ranging from $1.25 to $4.00.

Observations—Industries and care of the hive—

1. What is the hive, and what do wild bees use instead of the hive? Describe as follows:
2. Describe a brood chamber and a super and the uses of each.
3. How many and what bees live in a hive.
4. How the honey-comb is made and placed and the purpose of it.
5. How the wax is produced and built into the comb.
6. How honey is made.
7. What bee-bread is and its uses.
8. What propolis is and what it is used for.
9. How young bees look and how they are cradled and fed.
10. Does the removal of the honey from the supers in the fall do any harm to the bee colony?

11. How much honey should a good-sized colony have in the fall to winter well?

12. How should the hives be protected in the winter and summer?

What may be seen in the observation hive—

13. Describe how a bee works when building honey-comb.

14. How does the bee act when storing honey in a cell?

15. How does a bee place pollen in a cell and pack it into bee-bread?

16. Describe how the nurse bees feed the young, and how the young look when eating.

17. Describe how the "ladies in waiting" feed and care for the queen.

18. Try to observe the queen when she is laying eggs and describe her actions.

19. How do the bee workers keep their house clean?

20. How do they stop all crevices in the hive? If you keep the hive uncovered too long, how will they curtain the window?

21. Describe the actions of the bees when they are ventilating the hive.

22. If there are any drones in the hive, describe how they are fed.

23. How can you tell queens, drones and workers apart?

Honey bee with "tongue" partially extended

www.ingramcontent.com/pod-product-compliance
Lightning Source LLC
LaVergne TN
LVHW021331080526
838202LV00003B/140